Do ONLY what ... love

K,—d

Double Your Income Doing What You Love

Double Your Income Doing What You Love

RAYMOND AARON'S GUIDE TO POWER MENTORING

**Raymond Aaron
with Sue Lacher**

BICENTENNIAL

1807

WILEY

2007

BICENTENNIAL

John Wiley & Sons, Inc.

Published by John Wiley & Sons, Inc., Hoboken, New Jersey.
Published simultaneously in Canada.

Wiley Bicentennial Logo: Richard J. Pacifico

For general information on our other products and services or for technical support,
please contact our Customer Care Department within the United States at (800)
762-2974, outside the United States at (317) 572-3993 or fax (317) 572-4002.

Wiley also publishes its books in a variety of electronic formats. Some content that
appears in print may not be available in electronic formats. For more information
about Wiley products, visit our Web site at www.wiley.com.

Library of Congress Cataloging-in-Publication Data:

Aaron, Raymond.
    Double your income doing what you love : Raymond Aaron's guide to power
  mentoring / Raymond Aaron, with Sue Lacher.
        p.   cm.
    Includes index.
    "Published simultaneously in Canada."
    ISBN 978-0-470-17370-1 (cloth)
        1. Vocational guidance.   2. Success in business.   I. Lacher, Sue.   II. Title.
  HF5381.A22   2008
  650.1—dc22

                                                                        2007031693

Printed in the United States of America.
10   9   8   7   6   5   4   3   2   1

This book is dedicated to the thousands of Monthly Mentor™ members around the world who, by joining, have shown their dedication to continual learning and self-improvement. I applaud you for your willingness to take ownership and control of your life. May you live all your dreams! Also, it is through teaching you over these many years that I have been able to hone a program that allows you to double your income doing what you love, which is the subject matter of this book.

Also, this book is dedicated to you, my reader, for your desire to move forward in your life. You do not yet have the techniques to do more of what you love and less of what you do not love, but that process is revealed in the book that is in your hands right now. Devour it. Digest it. Savor it. Do the exercises detailed in this book. You will see your life inexorably moving forward in the exact direction of your choice.

Finally, this book is dedicated to the most important students I have in this lifetime— my sweet daughters, Juli-Ann Elizabeth and Emma Jacquelyn—who are also my greatest teachers.

Contents

Foreword

Do you know what your life's mission is? If you are like most people, you likely don't. But you probably have some things you love doing and long to experience more fully, goals you aspire to achieve, and dreams of how you would like your life to be. But again, if you are like most people, your life is likely filled with activities and obligations and commitments that have nothing to do with your goals or your dreams, your life's mission, or the things that you love. You may be spending your life running faster and faster just trying to keep up, and at the same time falling farther and farther away from living the life that you have always longed for.

Inspiring and empowering people to live their highest vision in a context of love and joy is the primary purpose of my life. I have made it my mission statement, and that commitment is clearly reflected in all areas of my business and personal life. Furthermore, it is an established fact that setting clear, well-written goals is a fundamental first step in moving toward creating the life you want, the one of your highest vision.

Raymond Aaron is a very successful man, and one reason is because he has discovered some powerful secrets about how this process of setting goals works. Over the last 24 years, he has developed, tested, and refined the stunning goal-setting and *goal-attaining* system outlined in this book. First, Raymond breaks life down into six pathways, and then sets out a masterful but simple system for you to set goals in all six categories every month. The forms he has created are easy to follow—each month you just sit down and fill in the blanks. As you follow his powerful system you will experience yourself beginning to achieve measurable successes, month by month. As you track your successes, you will see yourself begin to move ever closer to fully creating, and then living, the life you want, the life of your dreams.

I first met Raymond in the mid-eighties, and we liked and respected each other immediately. Raymond then supported me in my dream of creating the first *Chicken Soup for the Soul®* book by being one of our readers. Having recognized our goal of inspiring others through the power of story, he startled us by being the very first person to place a large order—1,700 copies of *Chicken Soup for the Soul* to share with his clients. This support ensured our early success, and helped launch us toward the huge success that *Chicken Soup for the Soul* eventually became. I was then honored to invite him to co-author two subsequent titles, *Chicken Soup for the Parent's Soul,* and then *Chicken Soup for the Canadian Soul.*

Recently, I invited a group of leaders who were doing transformational work to my home to share our ideas and best wisdom. I included Raymond, and as a group we were mesmerized when he began to share his goal-setting system. Each of us had done lots of goal setting, but his innovative presentation excited us all. We had all bumped up against the classic question of whether to set outrageous goals and risk failure, or set smaller goals and risk never going for the big ones. We were amazed to see how Raymond had solved this dilemma by teaching you how to set each goal at three levels: *M*inimum, *T*arget, and *O*utrageous. Using his *MTO*™ system, you can always have some level of success, and often it is the Outrageous success of your dreams! I was personally so impressed with this system that I have implemented it in my own office. My staff at Chicken Soup for the Soul Enterprises and Self-Esteem Seminars now use it, and each month we all set our goals using Raymond's unique goal-setting forms.

If you are mystified by the idea of having a life mission, one of Raymond's processes will help you to actually identify it—even if right now you have no idea what that statement even means. You can then begin to make good decisions about whom and what you want in your life, based on how they support, or don't support, your life's mission.

Most impressive to me is his process for helping you to identify the things that you love. After first identifying your "List of Loves," every month you can move closer and closer to the greatest gift of all—doing only what you love in your life.

Does this all sound like a lot? Well, you don't have to do it alone. This book will be your companion every step of the way. Once you have read it, go back and begin to work with it. The first step is always to take full ownership of your life and your future, rather than sitting back and simply letting it happen to you. Once you take charge, and accept full responsibility for everything in your life, you are free to begin designing and creating the life that you want! It takes courage, but it is your right if you want it, and you are designed by God to meet the challenge. And there is no greater accomplishment than moving forward and starting to live the life of your highest vision, in a context of love and joy. I wish you great success on your journey!

Jack Canfield
Co-creator,
Chicken Soup for the Soul®
and *The Success Principles*™

Acknowledgments

I am deeply honored to have around me friends, family, staff, colleagues, joint-venture partners, fellow teachers, and clients who have made such a valuable contribution to my life and to my life's work. This book and the Monthly Mentor™ program have, to a large extent, flowed out of their wisdom.

Whatever I am able to learn from them, combine with my own wisdom in unique ways, and then deliver to my clients through presentations, workshops, CDs, DVDs, web sites, subscription services, and this book, then enhances the lives of so many around the world. I feel blessed that I am this conduit. I am indeed deeply grateful. In particular:

- I thank Sue Lacher, the first person to work with me many years ago to bring the Monthly Mentor program to the world. She is now the Head Coach of the Monthly Mentor, a presenter on an important aspect of that program, and the co-author of this book.
- I thank my Director of Educational Events, Wendy Kuchar, who so powerfully organizes all our events so that I can concentrate on delivering the education.
- I thank my partner, accountant, controller, and general manager, Geoff Taylor, who handles all these diverse duties, and more, with calm, dignity, accuracy, and wisdom.
- I thank Alan Jacques for teaching me what has become the crucial *MTO* process that I now teach in the Monthly Mentor and in this book.
- I thank Janet Matthews who created the very idea of the Monthly Mentor program, encouraged me to switch careers to launch the program many years ago, and even named it for me.

- I thank our Customer Service Specialists, Lauren Atkinson and Courtney Schultz, for so enthusiastically and lovingly caring for and helping members of the Monthly Mentor and readers of this book from around the world.
- I thank Randy Wilson and Haruko Flower for creating such dazzling and effective multimedia for our educational products.
- I thank our Webmaster, Ashar Alam, for making our Internet presence such a helpful, convenient, and educational benefit.
- I thank Liz Ventrella and Tim Tiley for managing the flow of products from our production facilities and warehouse to our clients around the world.
- I thank Isobel Aaron for so dedicatedly running www .WealthCreatorSource.com so that subscribers around the world can enjoy listening to me interviewing a famous self-made millionaire or bestselling author every month.
- I thank our Accounting Department, Mikee Patel and Toni Perri, for keeping track of everything that happens in The Raymond Aaron Group™.
- I thank my Executive Assistant, Denise Harcourt, who has more than enough work to take care of me.
- I thank our Head Registrar, Ryan Malfara, for controlling the back of the meeting rooms so professionally that I can keep my attention fully focused on delivering great value to my clients.
- I thank those wonderful colleagues who invite me to teach these concepts to their clients: Bill Zanker and Samantha del Canto at the Learning Annex; Chris and Nicky Johnson at Free Money University; Scott and Ryan Scheel at Creative Commercial Real Estate; Larry Goins at Investor Palooza; Russ Whitney at The Wealth Intelligence Super Conference; Nicky Billou, Danish Ahmed, and Ash Silva; and DJ Richoux at Business Breakthrough Technologies. If they did not invite me, I could not reach so many people.

The End

HOW YOU CAN END YOUR OLD LIFE AND BEGIN USING "THE SECRET" LAW OF ATTRACTION

Congratulations! You have taken the first step. You have taken action. Just by taking this one step, you have acknowledged that you want a bigger future for yourself. You want to aim higher! You want more out of life. You want the *end of your old life*.

Whether you are an Olympic athlete going for Gold, a golfer determined to improve your game, a student working toward your degree, an up-and-coming entrepreneur wanting to launch a new business, or an individual motivated to lose weight, you've heard that when you focus your efforts on a specific outcome—a goal— you have a greater chance to bring it to fruition. This book guides you on a path that sup-

> *"You don't have to see the whole staircase, just take the first step."*
> —Martin Luther King, Jr.

ports the Law of Attraction. You will soon enjoy your dreams coming true, your goals achieving themselves *automagically*.

When it comes to setting goals, there are many different systems. They can be confusing, even daunting. I've heard from so many clients who have tried different systems and had no success whatsoever.

In this book, you now have a *proven method* to ensure that you achieve your goals effortlessly. You have found the answer. The search is over. You have everything you need within this book. Why am I so confident that you will succeed? Read what a few of my clients have to say by referring to the Appendix at the end of the book.

"Action is the foundational key to all success."

—Pablo Picasso

To read several more dazzling student testimonials plus one of the biggest lessons you'll learn from this whole book, you can also go to www.aaron.com/bonus.

You Need to Know Where You're Going

By recording your goals, you create your own personal roadmap. What is your destination? Do you know which road you will take? How long will it take to get there? What will you do if an obstacle comes along the way?

When you *forecast* the future, you are simply projecting a possible outcome. When you set a goal, you are actually *creating* your future.

Within this book you will be creating your personal roadmap and, yes, you will be redirected back on course if you lose your way. Remember, this is a proven method. You will find everything you need to achieve the success you desire.

Unwritten goals are just dreams. Writing your goals embeds them in your mind. This begins to call the Law of Attraction into play. You are making a commitment: *Yes, I want this. Yes, this is important to me.*

"Goals are dreams with deadlines."

—Diana Scharf Hunt

Yes, this is something worth striving toward. Once you record your goals, you begin to allow the Universe to do its part. You have clearly stated your intention. You have made a commitment. You implant a sensor within you to attract those things or individuals needed to help you along the way. You put the Law of Attraction into effect. Have you ever written a goal and then had things related to your goal just automatically show up from out of nowhere? That's the Law of Attraction working for you, fulfilling your dreams.

Goals keep you focused on your desired result. They help you make better decisions. They help guide you so that you are not a victim of circumstance, rather that you are making *conscious* choices.

When you record goals, you remove the chatter within your head. A sense of calm and focus takes over. You know where you want to go. You have a destination. You have a plan in place. Most important, you know the first step you need to take. You eliminate the dreaded,

"Someday I'll . . . ," by committing to a date and you step up to the plate by taking personal responsibility for your life.

It's not about blame, or the circumstances you came from. You might have had a great start, or you might not have been so fortunate. Don't let that stand in your way. When you think of successful individuals who have "made it," many have come from humble beginnings or have taken an

"Setting goals is the first step in turning the invisible into the visible."
—Tony Robbins

obstacle and actually used it to their advantage. Have you ever heard someone say, "Well, it's easy for him; he had a great start. His parents gave him everything. He was able to go to the university. I've always had to struggle to help make ends meet. Life has not been easy for me. Life is tough." Start today by taking responsibility for living the life you desire. Let those kinds of thoughts end.

If you are enjoying the quotes in this book, go to www.aaron.com/bonus to enjoy more of my very favorite quotations.

One Percent Equals One Hundred Percent

Your new life can be easy and effortless. Let the old one end.

Let's say you're controlling a motorboat and you're going south, and you want to go north. Will turning the rudder by 1 degree move you north? Yes—if you do it for a long enough time. If you make a 1 percent change for a long enough time, you'll

"The mind is like an elastic band; once stretched by a new idea, it never regains its original dimension."
—Oliver Wendell Holmes

be heading in the exact opposite direction sooner than you think. If you change your rudder by 1 degree, it doesn't take you years to change. Within a few minutes, even within half a minute, you are going 180 degrees in the opposite direction. You can make a 100 percent change in your life by making a 1 percent change in what you do. And once you make a 1 percent change, you never go back. Making small strategic changes marks the end of your old life.

A 1 percent change in what you do makes a 100 percent change in your life. You make little changes in your life and, within a few months, within a year, you'll be stunned; there will be hundreds of little "good" things you do that you never did before. There will be hundreds of "bad" things that you don't do any longer that you used to do. There will be hundreds of interactions, or people, or situations

> *"Desire is the key to motivation, but it's determination and commitment to an unrelenting pursuit of your goal—a commitment to excellence—that will enable you to attain the success you seek."*
> —Mario Andretti

that were unpleasant that just don't occur any longer, because a 100 percent change can occur from a 1 percent change in what you do *each minute.*

I have helped individuals like you around the world live the life of their dreams and experience the true joy of realizing goals that have deep meaning for them. Your goals are unique. For you, it may be realizing a childhood dream, or having financial freedom, or finding your perfect mate, or losing weight, or getting into shape, or becoming the top salesperson, or conquering personal or business challenges, or becoming skilled in your vocation. You will learn the 1 percent changes needed to end your old life and create the new life of your dreams.

Within this book, you have access to this unique system that has been honed, tested, and, most important, proven through the years. I have personally reaped the benefits and want to share my deepest wisdom with you. You now have a step-by-step guide so that you, too, can celebrate measurable progress each and every month and begin living your ideal life. Begin living on purpose and living by choice. Begin doing what you love and even doubling your income along the way. Does this sound good? It's proven—and the rewards await you.

Here Is What You'll Learn

Chapter 1: Have It Now! The Instant Gratification Society

How you can achieve your toughest goals right now without waiting

Learn a wonderful technique for getting whatever you want *right now.* You'll be invited to join the Instant Gratification Society—*without guilt.* This chapter presents possibly the most fascinating aspect of goal setting and goal achievement— namely that you can actually have whatever you want right now, no matter what.

Chapter 2: Your Annual Love Letters™

How you can move closer to what you love and further from what you do not love

How do you ensure that you do only what you love? Is it even possible? In this chapter, you will learn a unique process to reveal what is truly important to you in your life. Uncover what is missing from your life right now, so that you can correct these deficiencies. Start moving closer to what you love and further from what you do not love in order to live a life of joy and bliss.

Chapter 3: Your Life Missions™

How you can know exactly what you want to produce in this lifetime
You may be so caught up in the daily tasks of life that such an overview of your whole life, your *life purpose*, escapes you. Don't have a life of regrets. In this chapter, you will learn how to create a vision to pull you toward living a fulfilling and rewarding life. Learn how to focus your attention on moving toward what is truly important to you in this lifetime. Develop a strategy to focus your efforts on what you can do this year, even starting this month, toward your higher purpose.

Chapter 4: Your Special Talents

How you can enjoy the pleasure and heightened income of focusing your working life primarily on your special talents
What should you focus your energies on each day? What should you be spending your time doing? Of all the different tasks you could be doing today, which ones are the *best* ones for you to be focusing your attention on? When you were in school, you were told to work on and improve your weaknesses. I'll reveal why you need to focus on your strengths, which are those wonderful talents you have within you just waiting to be unleashed and improved. In this chapter, you'll crack the code of how you should spend your days and hours. Do you have *special talents*? Yes, you do. Uncover them and use them to propel you to new heights in your personal and professional life.

Chapter 5: Curing Procrastination Forever

How you can eliminate procrastination once and for all
You have procrastinated many times, even though you didn't want to. You may even procrastinate so regularly that your work, finances, or personal relationships suffer horribly because of it. In this chapter, you will learn the cure to procrastination so that you can blast through it once and for all—raising your self-esteem in the process. No more feeling bad that something didn't get done. No more nagging feeling in your gut. What a relief it is to eliminate procrastination

forever! Is this even possible? Absolutely, and the secret is revealed. Your old life is about to end.

Chapter 6: The Six MAINLY™ Pathways of Life

How you can create the richest and fullest possible life

There are six pathways of life. For a full and rich life, it is necessary to move forward every month in each one of these six pathways. What is a pathway? You may have heard of the traditional division of life into spiritual, family, financial, health, and so on. I have never found this division to be very useful, so I created six specific, useful pathways so that you can realize the success you deserve.

What happens if you don't know the six pathways and therefore do not take a forward step in each one monthly? The answer is that you become narrow and one-dimensional. When you learn to set a goal in each one of these six pathways, you find yourself striding confidently forward in your life. You find yourself following a holistic vision. You find yourself improving *synergistically*, with each aspect of your life helping all the other aspects. Your life becomes whole. What are the six pathways? Be open when you read them, because they will be radically different from what you have ever imagined. Learn about them in this chapter, and say goodbye to your old life.

Chapter 7: Achieve Your Goals for Sure

How you can achieve even your toughest goals no matter what— guaranteed!

In this chapter you will learn how to achieve any goal you record—*guaranteed!* Even more startling, you will learn how to achieve even your very toughest goals in some cases without doing any work at all. You'll find the concept introduced here to be absolutely revolutionary.

Chapter 8: The Six Goal-Recording Rules™

How you can record goals the right way so they effortlessly invoke the Law of Attraction

It is critically important to record goals correctly. Most people are not even aware there are rules. What are the rules for correct recording? I embarked on a groundbreaking research project to uncover, for the first time ever, the rules for recording goals correctly. There are huge lessons in this research for you. When you obey these rules, you will find that your goals begin to achieve themselves—*automagically*—because you will be correctly and powerfully invoking the Law of Attraction.

Chapter 9: Recording Goals So They Achieve Themselves Automagically

How you can employ the Law of Attraction to achieve your own goals, seemingly effortlessly

In this chapter, you will learn how to apply *The Secret Law of Attraction* when you record goals. When my mentored clients record their goals using the guidelines and forms developed within The Monthly Mentor™ program, their goals often achieve themselves. Sure, you should work on your goals; however, in addition to that, sometimes your dreams will just *show up.* The frequency with which your most outrageous goals will achieve themselves will shock you—when you record them on the special MAINLY form. You now get to combine everything you need to record your goals in a very special, effortless, and powerful way.

Chapter 10: Annual Backwards Goals™

How you can move strategically toward realizing even your biggest goals

Where do you envision yourself at the end of the year? What will you have achieved? How do you ensure your monthly goals line up with the bigger picture for the year? I teach my mentored clients how to write their yearly goals backwards. It may sound a bit silly; however, once something has been done, it is easier to do it the second time. You've probably heard the joke, "The second million is easier than the first, so I'm just going to start on the second million." It's a joke, but as in all humor, there's an element of truth. Read this chapter to unleash this powerful strategy to create the success you desire this year—and the years ahead!

Chapter 11: The Beginning

How you can ensure you achieve the success you desire for the rest of your mentored life

Rather than making New Year's Resolutions (that don't work), you will create your action plan for the year (that really does work). You will have a system in place to track your results, celebrate your successes, reap the benefits of a mentored life, build a team to support you, focus your efforts on doing only what you love, and double your income.

Raymond's Favorite Quotes

In my life, I have noticed that I can be moved and uplifted by intense connections with very special people, by powerful movies, and by special books. All of these take time, whether hours or years. But, the fastest way that I get inspired is by simply reading a famous quotation. Reading one such powerful sentence may take only a few seconds, but it uplifts my life for decades afterward. The following three quotations are among my most favorite and most moving:

Raymond's Comment: See what others do not, even if it is right in front of their eyes. They envision only bad weather and traffic jams, you see delightful possibilities. Expand your vision; widen your view; enhance your scope. When you do, magical snowmen will mysteriously appear in your life, while others grumble about shoveling.

"Snowmen fall to Earth, unassembled."
—Raymond Aaron

Raymond's Comment: It is way too easy to settle into a comfortable way of life, surrounding yourself with friends in that same place. It then seems to you that what you have created is reasonable and all your evidence proves that it is all you can likely achieve. Breaking out of your comfort zone unleashes powerful forces that will suddenly hoist you up into a place where higher souls dwell and more elevated achievements are the norm. Going to that new place is possible for you.

"Only those who risk going too far can possibly find out how far they can go."
—T. S. Eliot

Raymond's Comment: This is the motto for my own life. This is the quotation under my signature in all my e-mails. This is the worldview that turns me on. This is what brings the juice and zest into my life.

"Bite off more than you can chew, then chew like crazy."
—Crocodile Dundee

More of these quotes are sprinkled throughout the book. Furthermore, some very special quotes with an explanation of why they are so special are presented as a bonus at *www.aaron.com/bonus*.

Moving On

Are you ready? Let's begin.

CHAPTER 1

Have It Now! The Instant Gratification Society

HOW YOU CAN ACHIEVE YOUR TOUGHEST GOALS RIGHT NOW WITHOUT WAITING

If it's worth doing, it's worth doing *right now*.

I am sure you like this idea; I am also sure you can think of many things you want right now that you are sure you can't have, at least not right now. Well, what if there was a way that you *could* have those seemingly impossible things *right now*?

The good news is: There *is* a way. Before I tell it to you, first I need to point out a tiny disclaimer: *It's not perfect!* Yes, you will get whatever you want right now, *but it will be in a way that is slightly different from what you might imagine.* If you can handle that tiny condition, then get ready to begin creating new habits that will heighten your enjoyment of life. It will also bring those desirable long-term goals much closer.

Not only will you learn a wonderful technique to get whatever you want *right now*; you will be able to instantly apply it in your daily life.

Instant Gratification Is Good

First we need to address any concern you may have that instant gratification is not appropriate.

9

The good news is that you do not have to abandon *delayed* gratification. Yes, delayed gratification does have its rightful place. Unfortunately, you have been told it has the *only* place and that instant gratification has *no* place. That is not true. That mistaken belief will be corrected in this chapter. Not only will you know technically how to get instant gratification, but psychologically you will feel wonderful about it. You deserve it and you are worth it.

You can keep your membership in the Delayed Gratification Society. This chapter, though, invites you to be a *dual citizen*. You are hereby invited to join the Instant Gratification Society—*without guilt*.

The purpose of the Instant Gratification Society is not to mock those who plan. No, planning is good and is indeed the point of this book. Rather, the purpose of the Instant Gratification Society is:

- To give instant gratification its rightful place as one of the proper, legitimate, and respected possibilities
- To allow you to desire instant gratification without feeling guilty about it
- To teach you how to get what you want right now—*the right way*

This chapter presents possibly the most fascinating aspect of goal setting and goal achievement—namely that you can actually have whatever you want right now, no matter what, as long as you understand the disclaimer that you will *initially* get it in a way that is slightly different from what you now imagine.

This chapter is not going to give you permission to grab chocolate bars when you get hungry, or play hooky from work or school just because it is a sunny day. It is not about instant gratification for its own sake. It is about achieving your long-term goals right now, instead of waiting for many years.

Let's begin by using a fascinating example.

A Glorious One-Week Vacation Every Month

Can you think of one specific wonderful thing you'd like right now? I am sure you can. For the purpose of learning this technique, let's use an actual example from my own life so that you can easily understand how this fascinating technique works.

Several years ago, a colleague told me that he takes a glorious one-week vacation every month. I was intrigued by his plan. Of course, being at that time an unwitting member of the Delayed Gratification Society, I immediately dismissed the idea as bad, wrong, wasteful, and improper. When I tried to imagine myself having all those vacations, I was riddled with guilt thinking of my friends doing the "right" thing, working diligently. *No!* Such a laid-back life would not be for me.

As time progressed, I noticed that my colleague was a good man who did wonderful work in the world. He did not have any of the negative characteristics I thought to be associated with taking so many vacations.

I began slowly changing my ideas about instant gratification, but unfortunately it did take me years. It is the intention of this chapter to race you through those years I endured so that you can arrive quickly at the doorstep of the Instant Gratification Society.

> *"You can have anything you want right now, as long as you begin having it right now* in an abbreviated way."
> —Raymond Aaron

You can have anything you want right now, as long as you begin having it right now *in an abbreviated way.* This is real. It is certainly more real than hoping or dreaming or waiting. It is more real than denying that you could ever have it.

Let's first look at the obstacles to having so many vacations. When I first heard of the idea of a glorious one-week vacation every month, I definitely could not afford it. I certainly could not take so much time off work. My staff would be resentful. I would feel that I was wasting my time. My income would drop because I would have less time to work and I would have more expenses. I would lose clients because I would be away so often when they needed me. No, this was not a good plan. The obstacles were numerous and insurmountable.

In spite of all these perfectly reasonable obstacles, I began a process that was to carry me to goal-achievement beyond my wildest dreams. I began a process that actually allows me to achieve any goal I want, right now, no matter how long-term it really is.

Here is what I did. I decided that I would have a glorious one-week vacation beginning that very month—even if it wasn't *really* glorious and even if it wasn't *really* one week long. I know that this will at first seem strange to you. But stay with me.

My first such abbreviated one-week vacation was visiting my sister Susan for a Saturday. I did not call it a one-day visit. I called it my "glorious one-week vacation that month." Intellectually, I knew that it was only one afternoon long. But, emotionally, it felt great. I had embarked on my plan. I was not only thinking about it or working toward it, but, *in a real way*, I was already doing it.

On the drive home from my sister's place in the country, I let my mind fantasize about what my glorious one-week vacation would be next month. I decided that it would be a weekend skiing.

I enjoyed skiing so much that, on my way home from the ski resort, I planned my next glorious one-week vacation. Then, I found that I was planning my glorious one-week vacations many months in advance. Then, I realized that I was in the *habit* of taking glorious one-week vacations, even though they were, alas, abbreviated.

That's the key. I got into the *habit*. The possibility of having it in full reality became clearer and clearer in my mind. Huge changes were occurring in my mind, but also in the real world. Days were marked off in my calendar. Colleagues were hearing me talking about my glorious one-week vacations. They originally thought I was just being silly, but soon they realized that it was working. My world was *really* changing. I was getting closer. And, as I was getting closer, I was already enjoying *in some real albeit abbreviated way* exactly what I wanted.

Notice how powerfully the Law of Attraction was putting people and things into place for that dream to come true.

That first year, I succeeded in having *12* glorious one-week vacations. Two of them were indeed glorious and a full week long. Ten of them were abbreviated. But, in my mind, they were all glorious and in my imagination they were all one week long.

Now, I was a committed one-week-per-month glorious vacationer. My wife, at the time, got into the game, too. She began calling our outings "glorious one-week vacations." She enjoyed the thrill of planning our glorious one-week vacations and she did not seem to mind at all that they were usually abbreviated.

It was working. It was working not only in our minds, but also in our memories. Because we *called* each outing a "glorious one-week vacation" and because we cherished it and elevated it as we were experiencing it, in our memories it actually became a glorious one-week vacation.

But, it is even better than that. Within a few years, I had said the words so often that my staff was used to hearing these words and my clients were intrigued by the idea and the psychological obstacles had been smoothed away—and my wife and I were actually taking glorious one-week vacations every month and they really were truly glorious and they really were seven whole calendar days long. It had worked.

You may think that I take such vacations because I can afford them financially. But, most wealthy people take far fewer vacations than you imagine, because they feel the need to be close to work. Money is not what gets me all those vacations; it is the psychological preparedness that came from doing it so often, albeit in an abbreviated way, that has allowed me to take so many vacations.

In other words, I achieved my long-term goal only because I began it immediately in an abbreviated way. So, not only do you begin immediately to enjoy now an abbreviated version of your long-term goal, but in addition to that, beginning the abbreviated version now and implanting those habits actually brings the full version of the goal to reality much sooner.

One last word to you if you are still skeptical: Would you rather follow your current path of having maybe two or three one-week vacations a year, and have that forever, or would you rather at least *try* this approach? If you continue your own *reasonable* approach, you can expect to continue to have your two to three weeks of vacation a year. If you at least *try* my approach, you will instantly have 12 glorious one-week vacations, at least in your mind. And the habits will begin settling into your mind and your life.

In the next five years, I will have 60 glorious one-week vacations. Using your current plan, you will likely have maybe a half-dozen to a dozen such vacations. I guarantee that if you try my technique you will have 60 glorious one-week vacations in the upcoming five years—many of which will be abbreviated and a growing number of which will be real.

If you think this idea is great so far, wait till you hear the really good news. Here is the most startling aspect of this. Looking back over the years since I began the abbreviated glorious one-week vacations every month, some of my *best* memories were the *abbreviated* vacations, not the seven-day ones! It really works.

Now, let's use a totally different example—one that is related to cold hard cash.

Deposit $1,000 into Your Savings Account Every Month

Let's say that you have the same problem that many North Americans have: There is very little money left over at the end of each month. Putting your money into a savings account is not a strong investment. But, setting money aside instead of spending it all is a great habit to get into and to teach your children.

Would you like to be able to deposit $1,000 into a savings account each month? Would you like to be able to start that right now? Well, let's begin right now—of course, in an abbreviated way.

Commit to making a $1,000 deposit into a separate savings account on the first day of every month. If you are married, make a rule that you and your spouse go to the bank together to do this transaction. If appropriate, involve your children, too, so that they learn this valuable lesson.

As the beginning of next month gets closer, you (and maybe your spouse and children) begin thinking of how large your $1,000 deposit will be. Maybe you will decide that your $1,000 deposit will be $15. Okay; go to the bank on the first day of the next month and make your $1,000 deposit by depositing $15.

On the way home, talk about how wonderful it was that you succeeded for another month without fail to make your $1,000 deposit. Talk about how large next month's $1,000 deposit will be. Remember to always call it your "one-thousand-dollar deposit."

Maybe next month you will be able to have your $1,000 deposit be $200, the largest your $1,000 deposit has ever been up to that time. Celebrate your success.

Maybe one month you are totally broke. What should you do? I know for sure what you should do. The *habit* of making the $1,000 deposit on the first day of every month is far more important than the actual *dollar amount* of the deposit. So, go proudly to that bank, with your whole family if that works for you, and confidently deposit one dollar as your thousand-dollar deposit that month. Your self-esteem will skyrocket.

After five years of this, you will have made 60 "thousand-dollar" deposits. You will be in the habit. Your family will be in the habit. Your children will be making their own deposits. And I predict that at least one of those 60 deposits will actually be the full $1,000— perhaps more than one of them. How many real $1,000 deposits would you have made without this procedure?

More Examples of Having It Now

Hopefully you are quite intrigued by the possibility of having it now. How can this be applied in your life? Here are some examples:

Own an expensive sports car. Sit in that new car in the dealer showroom for a few minutes each month and call it your "ride in the country."

Own your own home. Walk through model suites each month admiring "the features of your own home."

Go on a once-in-a-lifetime two-month dream vacation. Let's say that it is a vacation to Greece. Then once per month, have a "Greece day" where you cook Greek food or rent a Greek movie like *Zorba the Greek* or go to a Greek restaurant or spend an evening with your mate learning some Greek language expressions or visit the Greek consulate in your city or go to the section of your museum about ancient Greece or learn the Greek alphabet. There are so many activities you could do. Make them fun. Be creative. The more you do this, the more the vacation will become real in your mind, and the less crazy such a dream vacation will be. Make sure to call these monthly activities your "once-in-a-lifetime two-month vacation to Greece." Here is how it sounds: "My 'once-in-a-lifetime two-month vacation to Greece' this month was learning the Greek alphabet."

Run a 10K footrace in one hour. Here's how I personally did it. I ran 1K in 6 minutes as my abbreviated way of completing my lofty goal. I told my friends that I had completed a 10K in one hour by running 1K today. Eventually they really got into the spirit with me. Next I accomplished 2K in 12 minutes as my 10K in one hour. Be careful, please. This is not a training technique on the topic of running; this is a mind game on the topic of goal accomplishment. It may not be the cleverest way to train your body to run a 10K in one hour, but it is the cleverest way to train your mind into thinking that you are an experienced 10K foot racer.

Do 100 sit-ups a day. You want to stay in shape by doing 100 sit-ups a day but you have a hard time getting past 25. So just do as many sit-ups as you can as long as you remember to announce that your 100 sit-ups that day were 25. When you are exhausted from a hard day at work, make sure you do at least one sit-up, as your 100 sit-ups that day, in order to keep implanting the habit.

Take a cruise once a year. Be creative in finding ways to do this in an abbreviated fashion. One year you might rent a paddle-boat for a day, or rent a canoe and go camping, or rent a rowboat, or go on a dinner cruise. The three requirements are that you keep doing this each year to get into the habit;

that you plan each year's outing with great fanfare to keep your dream in your memory; and that you call it your cruise for the year.

Maybe you've heard the famous story of the little boy who wanted a dog. His parents kept refusing. So, he decided one day that he already had a dog. Well, if he had a dog, he'd need a collar. He saved his paper-route profits and bought a collar. His parents were confused. Then he bought a leash; then a food dish; then some dog toys. He was so clear in his mind that he had a dog that he told the pet store owner and all his friends about his little dog and all the accessories he had acquired for his dog. The crowning glory came when he actually named his dog and bought a dog tag. It will be no surprise to you that his parents one day showed up with a puppy for him. What else could they possibly do?

These are powerful examples of invoking the Law of Attraction.

The Five-Step Technique for Having It Now

Here are the five steps. Follow each one exactly as stipulated to ensure that it works for you.

1. *Select one long-term goal* that you really want right now.
2. *Decide on the abbreviated version* that you will begin enjoying. In other words, decide on how you will begin achieving it right now, in an abbreviated way. Sometimes it is easy to figure out the abbreviated version. Sometimes you will need to be quite creative to figure this out.
3. *Tell at least one other person* about your plan. Telling more people is even better. Be careful to tell only supportive and positive people. You may wish to ask those special people to read this chapter. Supportive positive people will be able to help you through the tough times that will definitely come. This is a mind game so you must protect your mind!
4. *Do the first abbreviated action immediately*, so that you are in the game.
5. *Celebrate your success every time* you do the abbreviated action and remember to always refer to it as the full action. In other words, remember to say, for example, "My one-thousand-dollar deposit this month was seventeen dollars and I deposited it on time as usual."

I want to celebrate your success. Please tell me all about your success at www.aaron.com/bonus and I will send you a gift to help you have even more successes.

FAQs

1. **Is this for real, or is it just a mind trick?**

    It starts as a mind *game,* not a trick. You are an adult. You are not really tricking yourself, but you are initially playing a game. Once the game becomes more real, you will notice that you occasionally do get the *real* thing—not the abbreviated version—and you may get it far more often than you at first imagined.

    Furthermore, sometimes an abbreviated achievement can give you more pleasure and benefit than the far-in-the-future real one. Imagine the huge leap of self-esteem when you make even a tiny $1 deposit as your $1,000 deposit one month, even though you were totally broke. That one stand may give you more character and growth than actually making a full $1,000 deposit, years into the future.

2. **Does this mean that eating that extra dessert is a good idea, just because you want it now?**

    No. The technique of having it now is a procedure for bringing forward in time, right to the present, a long-term goal that you rationally know you cannot attain for years—maybe never. It is a way to achieve your dreams right now, even if you know intellectually that it is not really possible. It is a way to get into the *habit* of already having what you rationally know you cannot yet have.

3. **Is there a way that having it now will not work?**

    Yes, there is, unfortunately, a very real way that it will not work for you. If you begin missing thousand-dollar deposits, if you begin missing abbreviated one-week vacations, then the formation of the essential habit is destroyed or at least severely lessened. In that case, no one (not even you) will believe it and it will not come true.

    This technique is based on forming a habit (which is real). It is based on your family, friends, and co-workers getting used to your behavior. It is based on consistency. It is based on doing the job as you have promised to yourself, exactly when scheduled, no matter how abbreviated. If you do not create this habit, you will not get the benefit.

Go right now to www.aaron.com/bonus to see a bonus video where I personally teach you some fascinating extra lessons on the *Instant Gratification Society*. And, I just may have a gift for you there!

Three Expert Action Steps

In this chapter, you learned that you have been a lifetime member of the Delayed Gratification Society, possibly without even realizing it. You have been invited to *also* join the Instant Gratification Society. You now hold *both* memberships, so you can plan for a wonderful long-term future *and* you can have as much as you wish of that long-term future right now. You know that it is a mind game initially, but that it quickly becomes real both in your mind and in the universe. You know that your family members will quickly learn to enjoy this game and will support you in it, if you are dedicated to consistency. You know that you can fail at it by slipping out of consistency. Since it is a mind game, you know that you need to enjoy it in your mind as it is becoming real for you and others in the real world.

It is time to use what you have learned. Below are listed the *Three Expert Action Steps*™ designed to best support you in bringing what you have just read into play in your life. Once you have completed these Three Expert Action Steps, you will be ready to move on to the next chapter, which will support you in dramatically increasing the joy in your life.

> **First Expert Action Step: Select one long-term goal you wish to begin enjoying right now.**
> Once you have selected your goal, follow the five-step technique exactly as outlined earlier in this chapter.

> **Second Expert Action Step: Plan more uses of this technique.**
> As soon as you have seen success with this technique in the long-term goal of the First Expert Action Step, immediately go to www.aaron.com/bonus and tell me all about your success. As promised, I will send you a gift. Then, make a list of other long-term goals you wish to enjoy right now. *Caution:* Do not begin a second program for at least three to six months,

to allow your mind to set in place the habits from your first long-term goal.

Third Expert Action Step: Enroll others into the Instant Gratification Society.

Tell your colleagues, friends, or children about this fascinating way to get what might otherwise take them years to get. Teach them this technique so that they can have more success—sooner. Let them read this chapter. Invite them to enjoy a special brief video presentation on Instant Gratification at www.aaron.com/bonus. They will get a gift, too!

Moving On

Now that you can achieve even tough long-term goals instantly, it is time to add more joy to your life by learning about love. It's time to have more love in your life and the next chapter shows you how, step by step.

CHAPTER

2

Your Annual Love Letters

HOW YOU CAN MOVE CLOSER TO WHAT YOU LOVE AND FURTHER FROM WHAT YOU DO NOT LOVE

Surely you want to do more of what you love and less of what you don't love. You are about to learn how to do exactly that. And I promise I will personally help you at a special web site created just to ensure you do a great job on your Annual Love Letters™.

"I love this so much, I'd do it for free!"

You've heard people say this. You may even have said it yourself. It sounds wonderful, but it is a tragic error. It totally misses the whole point of life and work. What this dreamy-eyed person is saying is that it is okay to be unhappy at work as long as you are happy outside of work. Just struggle through any lousy job to put food on the table and then have a real life when no one is looking. That's not the path I want for myself, or for my mentored clients around the world—or for you.

> "I get to play golf for a living. What more can you ask for—getting paid for doing what you love."
>
> —Tiger Woods

A far better statement is: "I love this so much, it is the *only* thing I will do for money."

Now, that's a fulfilling life! That is a path to strive for. That is a noble pursuit. Do you want to get there? I am sure you do. The first step is knowing exactly what you love. Specifically, you need

> *"What you would do willingly for free is the only thing you should ever do for money."*
>
> —Raymond Aaron

a comprehensive, unedited, and uncensored list of your loves. This chapter presents an intriguing and novel way to create such a list for yourself.

Creating a List of Loves That Is Real

What Is Meant by an "Unedited and Uncensored" List?

If you were asked right now to make a list of your loves, you would first think of a love—maybe your dog. Then, your *inner censor* would take over. It would scream into your ear: *Better record your spouse first, before your dog, or else you may get into big trouble.* Again, just as you are about to record one of your dearest lifelong friends as another one of your loves, your inner censor leaps in to save you from another social blunder by reminding you: *Better record all of your friends so no one feels left out.*

Now you are worrying about social blunders and others' feelings. There is a time and place for propriety. But, now is not the time or the place. Why? Because if you *pretend* or *try* or *hope* to record a list

> *"Most people are other people. Their thoughts are someone else's opinions, their lives a mimicry, their passions a quotation."*
>
> —Oscar Wilde

of loves, but really just record a list of socially correct and politically proper things, you will be doomed to a life of pretence and façade. Your life will become one of to-do lists and social obligations, instead of a life filled with true joy.

This is the time to be ruthlessly honest with yourself. This is the time to stake out a territory inside your own head. This is a time to clearly proclaim: "This is my territory. This is where I wish to live for the rest of my life. These are my own real true loves."

To support yourself in this honesty, you may wish to keep your Annual Love Letters a *private* document, not to be seen by others.

I want you to look truthfully into your own life. What do I mean? Well, think of what you love:

- Do you love reading? If so, when did you last sit down and enjoy reading a good book? A year ago? Five years ago? When you were in school? If you love reading and you are not reading, then whose life are you living?

- Do you love travel? Are you traveling as much as you wish?
- Do you love your grandchildren? Do you see them as often as you wish?

To drive this point home even more clearly, let me relate an incident that happened while I was coaching a young couple in The Monthly Mentor™ program who had to make a very important life decision. The husband had lost his job months before and had diligently sought new employment.

Then he was unexpectedly offered two different jobs at the same time. To make matters worse, both potential employers needed a quick decision. The jobs were in different fields. They offered different titles, different salaries, and different potential for improvement in the future. One required a move to another city, but had a higher starting salary. The other had a lower starting salary but better benefits and greater potential—if certain conditions were met.

On and on the couple explained the many different and conflicting issues related to this tough decision. They finally completed their presentation to me.

I simply asked them on which grounds were they going to make their decision. In other words, what are the most important criteria to take into account? Instead of looking at the characteristics of the jobs, I asked them to look *first* at what they themselves really wanted out of life and out of work.

They were stunned by my suggestion. They looked at each other quizzically, not knowing how to decide what the criteria were that they should use. This, by the way, is a very common problem. I have seen this consistently among unmentored souls drifting around wondering what is important.

I told them to do the Annual Love Letters process that you are about to learn in this chapter. When they had each completed their lists of loves, I asked them to look at their loves and to look at the two different job opportunities and base their decision on their loves. The smiles on their faces exuded a dazzling light of happiness as clarity suddenly got turned on in their life.

One job would have caused eventual frustration and unhappiness as it contained nothing that either wanted—but it was the higher starting salary (which they admitted had been swaying them).

The other was perfect, but it was perfect only *after* they realized that they should be making decisions based on their loves.

It is easy to get distracted by "stuff" like a health benefits package, a prestigious title, a fancy office, and so forth. As shallow as this stuff may seem, it is extraordinarily compelling in real life. Why? Because it seems to declare that you have attained a high station in life to deserve such rewards. It is not just creature comforts; it is a proclamation to society that you have arrived. This is hard to ignore.

"One of the most tragic things I know about human nature is that all of us tend to put off living. We are all dreaming of some magical rose garden over the horizon—instead of enjoying the roses that are blooming outside our windows today."

—Dale Carnegie

But, the downside of going against your loves to grab this stuff is such consequences as divorce, unhappiness, addictions, affairs, future job losses, illnesses, and so on. Go for love, not for "stuff."

You are now getting the point. The point is to ensure that you are totally *in* your own life. How do you get in? By doing only what you love.

The threefold purpose of the exercises in this chapter is for you:

1. To have an uncensored, unedited list of your loves, so that you have a clear, written record of what is truly important to you in your life.
2. To realize what is missing from your life right now, so that you can correct these deficiencies.
3. To help you prioritize your goals based on what you love, so that you move closer to what you love and further from what you do not love.

Let's do it. Let's make the list. Your important first step is to have in front of you a special form called *Annual Love Letters* (see Figure 2.1). You can obtain a copy of this form in two ways:

1. Photocopy the Annual Love Letters form in Figure 2.1. Unfortunately, it is smaller than normal because of the size of the pages of this book and may be a little inconvenient to use.
2. Surf into www.aaron.com/DoubleYourIncome, which is the official web site for readers of this book to download a full-size, full-color, printer-friendly copy of this special form.

ANNUAL LOVE LETTERS™
LIST OF CURRENT LOVES

THE
MONTHLY
Mentor™

① My Name _____   ② Today's Date _____

	PAST		PRESENT						FUTURE

PAST

③ My Loves
④ Why Important

PRESENT

⑤ Importance (H,M,L)
⑥ Last Time (D,M,Y)
⑦ Devoting Time And Energy (H,M,L)
⑧ Money Needed ($)
⑨ Choose To Do (Date)

FUTURE

⑩ First Step

	③ My Loves	④ Why Important	⑤ Importance (H,M,L)	⑥ Last Time (D,M,Y)	⑦ Devoting Time And Energy (H,M,L)	⑧ Money Needed ($)	⑨ Choose To Do (Date)	⑩ First Step
A	I love							
B	I love							
C	I love							
D	I love							
E	I love							
F	I love							
G	I love							
H	I love							
I	I love							
J	I love							
K	I love							
L	I love							
M	I love							
N	I love							
O	I love							
P	I love							
Q	I love							

⑪ My Signature _____

⑫ Insights Gained: 1. _____
2. _____
3. _____

Figure 2.1   Annual Love Letters Form

25

Now that you have either photocopied or downloaded this form, you need to personalize it by printing neatly your name and today's date. Please include the year in the date, because you will want to redo this exercise annually and it will be very enlightening for you to look back over your lists from previous years to see how your own life is changing.

Put the form and pen aside while we first do a verbal exercise. This verbal exercise requires help from a friend or family member. It will take only a few minutes.

Here is what the two of you are to do:

1. Have your friend yell quickly at you: "What do you love?"
2. Then you yell back as fast as you can, without thinking, one thing you love.
3. Your friend then yells back: "What do you love?"
4. Again, you reply.
5. Keep this up until you slow down in thinking of new loves, which will likely be about 10 to 15 answers.

There are several important points to be made about this exercise so that it works correctly. First, your friend must *not* give you enough time to think about your answer. Your friend must keep yelling that question at you so rapidly that you just *barely* have enough time to blurt out an answer. Why? Because if you are forced to yell out an answer without time to think, then your inner censor cannot slip in with its insidious thoughts of social correctness.

Another important point to keep in mind is that it is okay to say whatever comes to mind—even if it seems silly. For example, let's say that you blurt out "dancing" as one of your loves. Well, maybe you haven't danced since school. Maybe you have never danced in your life. Maybe you always refuse to go dancing when your spouse suggests it. So, it is irrational to yell "dancing." But, we are not interested in rationality or correctness or censorship. We are interested in your innermost soul getting a voice—as unexpected as the answers may seem.

Keep in mind that just because you blurt out a love verbally does not mean that you are required to record it on your written list of loves. This is just an exercise to help you uncover your loves *verbally*. There is no commitment in the *verbal* part of this exercise. Remember that you blurt out your replies; you do *not* record them during this exercise. At least, you do not record them *yet*.

You may repeat an answer. Why? Because the point is to keep answering for as long as you can without pause or silence. So, fill silence with an answer, even if you have already given it. It keeps up the momentum.

By the time you slow down in thinking of answers, you will have spoken about a dozen loves that came out of your innermost soul, without censorship. It is important now to keep silent. Sit down calmly. Be contemplative.

Ponder what has just happened:

- Have you blurted out some loves that you had not thought of for a long time?
- Have you blurted out some loves that do not make any rational sense to you?
- Have you blurted out some loves that make huge sense to you but that you had been ignoring or submerging for a long time?

Take time now to consider what you have just learned about yourself and your life.

After a discreet period of being pensive, take up your pen and enter the loves you choose to record in column #3, entitled "My Loves" on the Annual Love Letters form. Go *down* the first column, not across the form. The purpose now is simply to *capture* your loves on paper in writing. You will analyze each one, after you have recorded them all. Just print your loves neatly down that column in whatever order they come to your mind. Keep silent; the responses that you gave out loud are only a guide. If there's something that you said that you don't want to write down because it's not really a love, you just said it on the spur of the moment, that's fine. And if there's something that you *now* think of that you didn't say out loud, that's fine, too. The verbal part was just a memory jogger.

The order is not important. Just record your loves without thought as to which is first, which is second, and so on. You will prioritize them after you have captured them.

Take your time. *Print neatly.* These are your loves.

When you have completed printing your loves on the Annual Love Letters form, sit quietly again and review this list. As you are reviewing this list, more ideas may come to you. Add them. The order of recording is not important.

To invoke the Law of Attraction, you must use your mind and your heart. This exercise helps you bring your heart into play.

Analyzing Your List of Loves

Now you have a list of loves. As this is the first time you have done the Annual Love Letters exercise (see Figure 2.2), it is unlikely that you will have captured all your loves. That's the bad news. The good news is that this process is so powerful you can be assured you have captured the majority of them, certainly the most significant ones.

Once you have completed recording your loves, go to column #4, which is labeled "Why Important."

Once you have your list of lettered loves, indicate why each love is important to you. You might have listed "dog," because "He gives me a feeling of being welcome when I come home." For "vacations" you might record, "They rejuvenate me." In other words, print neatly in heartfelt words why that particular love is important to you.

When you finish column #4, go to column #5. Rate the relative importance of each of your loves. Here's how to do it: Mark each love that is of High Importance with an *H*. Do not record every love as High Importance. I want you to discern. I want you to distinguish among them, and that means going down the column and just recording the capital letter *H* beside those loves that are truly of High Importance to you.

The next step is to go down that same column and write down an *L* for those loves that are of Low Importance for you. You might have written down, "I love sunrises." Well, maybe you do, but if you see only one a year, that may actually be fine by you. And if you don't see one, maybe it's not that critical. You might put an *L* for Low Importance beside that one.

And the final step, for those loves that are still blank, is to write down an *M* for Medium Importance.

Next, go to column #6, which is labeled "Last Time." You will notice there is a *D*, an *M*, and a *Y* under it. Let me explain what that means. I want you to look at each love and determine the last time you actually experienced that particular love. If it was recently, in other words, days ago or maybe a week or so ago, write down a *D* for *Days*. If it was months ago or one or two seasons ago, write down an *M* for *Months* ago. If it was a long time ago, record a *Y* for *Years* ago.

PURPOSE:

- To have a written list of your loves
- To realize what you're missing
- To help you prioritize your goals

BENEFITS:

- **so that you** ...... will have a clearer record of what is important to you in your life.
- **so that you** ...... can change this.
- **so that you** ...... ensure you get what you want in your lifetime.

Please Follow These INSTRUCTIONS:

A. Neatly print your ① Name and ② Today's Date.

B. Have a friend say to you "What do you love?" You **immediately** respond "I love..."
   Repeat this process over and over **quickly** until you run out of ideas. Rules for this process are:
   - Do not write anything, just respond.
   - Repeat a previous answer, if you must.
   - Respond quickly without thinking.
   - Do not censor your answers.

③ Keep silent. Remember to use your responses only as a guide. In any order, record your Loves. Add whatever new Loves come to mind.

④ Once you have your list of lettered Loves, indicate why they are important to you.

⑤ Rate their relative Importance to you. Mark each Love of High Importance with an H. Mark each Love of Low Importance as L. Mark all others as M for Medium.

⑥ Record the last time you experienced this love by recording a D if it was within days, M if it was within months, or Y if it was years ago.

⑦ Rate the amount of time and energy you are currently devoting to each Love by rating it as H, M, or L.

⑧ Record the amount of money required, if any, to experience each Love.

⑨ Record the date you choose to experience each Love.

⑩ Record the First Step required for the Love you choose to experience. You can choose to focus, for example, on three of your Loves recording the First Step. Once you have experienced these, you can go back and select more of your Loves to focus on.

⑪ Sign your name to show your commitment to yourself.

⑫ Record your Insights Gained from this process.

SAMPLE:

			PAST			PRESENT			FUTURE	
	③ MY LOVES	④ WHY IMPORTANT	⑤ IMPORTANCE (H,M,L)	⑥ LAST TIME (D,M,Y)	⑦ DEVOTING TIME AND ENERGY (H,M,L)	⑧ MONEY NEEDED ($)	⑨ CHOOSE TO DO (DATE)	⑩ FIRST STEP		⑪ MY SIGNATURE
A	I love being creative	contributing something new	L	M	L	395	Feb.10	enroll in marketing course		
B	I love swimming	maintain fitness	H	Y	L	500	Feb.1	renew membership at fitness club		
C	I love seeing sunrises	starting day off with gratitude	L	D	H	0				
D	I love traveling	enjoy new experiences	M	Y	L	2500	Feb.2	book family vacation		
E	I love my son	being a great dad	H	D	M	0				
F	I love my wife	being a great husband	H	D	M	0				

⑫ INSIGHTS GAINED: 1. _Hire an assistant to help me so that I can take more vacations_
2. _Block days in my calendar to do something special with my son_
3. _Pay more attention to my health and wellness_

Figure 2.2 Completed Annual Love Letters Sample

This will help you understand where your loves rate with respect to whether you are experiencing them.

So far, everything that you've done is within the master category labeled *Past.* These are the loves that you've experienced in the past, why they are important to you, their level of importance, and then how long ago.

Column #7 is the only column that relates to the *Present* and that's "Devoting Time and Energy." Here you will rate the amount of time and energy you are *currently* devoting to each love by rating it as an *H, M,* or *L.* Put an *H* beside those loves that are High in "Devoting Time and Energy." Maybe you spend lots of time with your children—that would be High; maybe you rarely see a sunset, so you would write Low; and everything else is Medium. Go down the column putting in the *H*s, then go down the column putting in the *L*s, and finally go down the column and just complete any cell that is empty with the letter *M.*

Now you will go into your *Future,* which is the most exciting part. Column #8 is "Money Needed." Write down an estimate of how much money is needed to experience this love. Maybe to enjoy your dog, you don't need much money; maybe to enjoy a sunset, you don't need any money; but maybe to go on vacation you need $5,000. There's a little bit of flexibility here. Of course, no one knows in advance how much a vacation is. It depends on where you go, how long you stay, and how many people go with you, but just record roughly the dollar amounts so that you can actually see which ones of your loves require spending money and which do not.

The next column is #9, the "Choose to Do (Date)." From the entire list, select *three* loves that you want to experience more fully. Of course, you want to experience all your loves, but if you look down the list you'll notice there are some loves that you are not experiencing as fully as you wish to. Choose three of them, and in column #9, write down the date that you are actually going to do something about that particular love.

Then in column #10, record the "First Step" that you are going to take. Record the first step required for you to experience that love.

Now, #11 is your signature at the very bottom.

In the box labeled #12, record the insights that you gained from doing this exercise. I would like to jog your thinking to help you. I am going to ask you some rhetorical questions. You don't have to answer each one, but they're going to jog your thinking so that you will come up with insights that you have gained from doing this. I'm going to actually go from left to right across the page.

When you recorded your loves, did you notice that they were easy to identify? Were they easy to record or did you struggle to find them? Just *notice;* there's no right or wrong, or good or bad. Record that insight.

In the next column, was it easy for you to determine why those loves were important? Or was it hard for you? Record that insight.

In the next column, level of importance, did you record all your High Importance loves at the top? Were the High Importance loves the very first ones in your mind, or are they all at the bottom, meaning it took you a while to get down to them? Or are they just scattered randomly throughout, meaning that before you did this exercise you had no idea which were your most important loves and which were not? Record this insight.

What about the last time you experienced these loves—were they all days ago? Are there many of them that are months and years ago? Are some of your High Importance loves months and years ago? How does that make you feel? What insights did you get from that? Record this insight.

Now, in the present, how much time are you devoting? Are you devoting High, Medium, or Low energy and time to most of your loves or very few of them? And if it's only very few, are you devoting your time and energy to your High Importance loves? The hallmark of a mentored life is that you focus on what is truly important to you. Record your insights.

Now, let's go into the future. Is there a lot of money needed for some of your loves? How can you get that money? Or is there very little or no money needed to experience the loves that you truly want to experience, and yet maybe you haven't experienced them for months or years? What does that mean? Record your insights.

For the three that you've chosen to experience more fully, are they the High Importance loves? Did you choose to experience the High Importance loves or not? Is the first step doable? And here's the big thing: Take what you recorded as the first step in column #10 and make a commitment to take that first step. You will learn how to make that commitment in subsequent chapters of this book.

> *"An unexamined life is not worth living."*
>
> —Socrates

Ponder these insights. They are huge insights. They are at the very center of your life. They are truly where you live—or want to live.

Record these precious insights. They are a statement of exactly where you are right now in your own life.

Without this introspection, you are doomed to live an unexamined life filled with the dailyness and noises of life—and not filled with the true joys of your life.

Using the List to Improve Your Life

Take a blank sheet of paper and entitle it, "Future Actions." Date it. On this sheet of paper, you are to record every action you could take now or in the future in order to alter your life in ways suggested by this Annual Love Letters exercise.

> *"Doing what you love is the cornerstone of having abundance in your life."*
>
> —Wayne Dyer

Here are some questions that may help you determine what actions you could take:

- What loves are missing from your list that you would like to add? How do you intend to do that? And when?
- Is there some way you wish to change the prioritizing of your loves into H, M, and L? How do you intend to do that? And when?
- Which loves do you wish to more fully experience right now or very soon? How do you intend to do that? And when?
- What has caused you sadness, regret, or feelings of failure while doing this exercise? How do you intend to correct that? And when?
- What other insights have you gained that give you ideas as to what you can do now to improve your life? How do you intend to do that? And when?

A mentored life is one in which you are asked, by your mentor, to ponder such deep questions.

FAQs

1. **Why is the word *annual* in the Annual Love Letters?**

   The word *annual* is important because it reminds you that this process must be repeated yearly. In The Monthly Mentor program, this is one of the cornerstone processes that we redo each year. My mentored clients report huge insights, not just from doing this exercise, but from *redoing* it. They say that it is only because they were asked to redo the exercise that they, somewhat reluctantly, did it. But, then they noticed startling changes in their successive lists from year to year that were totally unexpected and positive. Life does change. Loves do change. As you mature and move closer to what you love and farther from what you do not love, other mountaintops become visible that were previously obscured from the lower vantage point you used to have.

2. **How can loves change? Don't I come *hardwired* with certain specific loves?**

   You change when your hobbies change; when you marry or divorce; when children and grandchildren are born; when you study different courses; when your job or whole career change; when you get involved in certain causes in the world; when you have accidents, illnesses, or other setbacks; when you meet new people; when you are moved by a book, movie, or documentary. Yes, these influences have the capability to make profound changes in your life and hence in your loves. Otherwise, life would be stagnant.

3. **Do I really need someone to yell "What do you love" for this to work?**

   Yes. It may seem unnecessary but, without this pressure, you will definitely fall victim to recording your social obligations and political correctness. From that feeble base, no strong house can be built.

   Can Raymond himself help me do this exercise? Yes. If you do not have a close friend to do this with, simply go to www .aaron.com/DoubleYourIncome and I will personally help you. I will explain the entire process to you and I will personally yell "What do you love?" for you. Go there now. I want to help you do it right.

4. **Is it important whom you choose as the person to yell "What do you love"?**
Yes. Be very careful to select someone with whom you can be totally honest. If you are considering asking your spouse to volunteer, you need to first ensure that your spouse will not be upset by any of your responses. Or, worse, will you be censoring your answers to gain your spouse's favor or attempt to not upset your spouse? Will some of your loves possibly offend the beliefs of your questioner? Be careful to select the right person who will allow you to be free in your mind to be totally honest. If you have any worries at all, it may be safer for you to let me do it for you at www.aaron.com/DoubleYourIncome.

5. **Is it bad to realize that I am not experiencing the majority of my own loves?**
No, it is not bad. It is usual, in an unmentored life. If everyone instinctively did only what they loved and if everyone was already fully experiencing their most significant loves, there would be no need for this revealing exercise. It is revealing because we tend to get caught up in the daily routine of life and sometimes miss the bigger picture.

   Though it is not bad to be fully experiencing only a few of your loves, it is definitely not okay to let this sad state persist. Now that you have deeply and honestly examined your life, now that you have made these revelations, it is not okay to let a less-than-optimum situation persist. You may experience right now a rush of desire to do something about this situation.

6. **There are certain financial realities in life. How can I be assured that going toward my loves will also fulfill my financial needs?**
In this chapter, you have certainly learned that striving for the *stuff* will give you the financial benefits, but will lead to disastrous consequences like illness, sadness, divorce, affairs, midlife crises, errors, accidents, and so on. So, aiming for the stuff is a short-sighted and doomed way to run your life.

   Now, let's look at the other side of the coin. Will following your loves guarantee you the financial benefits? I cannot guarantee this in every case. But, I have seen it happen so often with so many of my mentored clients that I can do nothing else but strongly recommend this course of action for your life.

Here is a delightful paradox. When you go for love, one of the amazing side-benefits is that you often get all the stuff. And, even better, you may well get *more* of it than if you directly went for the stuff.

7. **In the whole scheme of an examined, mentored life, where do loves fit?**
   Think of life as a pathway. You begin somewhere and you are going somewhere. Your loves are where you come *from*. Your Life Mission is where you are going *to*. So, in the whole scheme of an examined life, knowing your loves and committing to running your life *from* your loves is half the answer. The other half is where you are going *to*. That answer will be discovered in the next chapter.

   Be sure to do this fascinating exercise with a friend or by letting me personally help you at www.aaron.com/Double YourIncome.

Three Expert Action Steps

You know how to create your own uncensored and unedited list of loves. You know to prioritize your list. You have learned how to analyze the list. You know you will make important decisions as to which loves you will pursue more fully. You know you will record many insights. You know you will make commitments as to what actions you will take.

It is time to use what you have learned. Below are listed the Three Expert Action Steps™ designed to support you in bringing what you have just read into play in your life. Once you have completed these Three Expert Action Steps, you will be ready to move on to the next chapter, which will help you to gain a clear vision of where you wish to go in your life.

   First Expert Action Step: Complete the exercises suggested in this chapter.
   To complete the Annual Love Letters, either photocopy the form in this chapter or download a full-page full-color form from www.aaron.com/DoubleYourIncome. Complete

it using the instructions in this chapter as your guide. Ask a friend to help you or let me help you at www.aaron.com/DoubleYourIncome. Then, record your insights as suggested and record your own ideas for action, as also suggested.

Second Expert Action Step: Select the three loves you wish to experience more fully and decide how you will go about implementing the first step in the process.
Though it may be a multistep process to actually arrive at that place, what is the *first step* you could take today or this week to move you closer to fully experiencing those loves? Record that step and do it!

Third Expert Action Step: Make entries in your calendar to ensure you are successful at these tasks.
Make entries in your calendar to:

- Redo this exercise in December every year, so that you are ready for the New Year.
- Check to see if the first step you set in the Second Expert Action Step has been accomplished.
- Remind yourself in three months to review your Annual Love Letters to keep them in the forefront of your mind.

By doing this, it is more likely that you will make critical decisions in your life based on your loves. In this way you will invoke the powerful Law of Attraction.

Moving On

Congratulations. You know where you must come from. The next chapter will help you identify where you are going.

CHAPTER 3

Your Life Missions

HOW YOU CAN KNOW EXACTLY WHAT YOU WANT TO PRODUCE IN THIS LIFETIME

She was a little startled by seeing the Cheshire Cat sitting on a bough of a tree a few yards off. The Cat only grinned when it saw Alice.
"Would you tell me, please, which way I ought to go from here?"
"That depends a good deal on where you want to get to," said the Cat.
"I don't much care where," said Alice.
"Then it doesn't matter which way you go," said the Cat.
                            —Lewis Carroll, *Alice in Wonderland*

I have included this excerpt from Lewis Carroll's *Alice in Wonderland* so that you can begin asking yourself where you are going in this lifetime.

Because you are reading this book, I know that this question is very important to you. You want to know where you are going. You desire this clarity. I applaud you. Unfortunately, most people do not even ask this question. As a result, when you have a clear answer to this question you will be well ahead of most others. You will be able to steer your life in the direction you truly wish to go.

This *direction* is called your *life mission*.

Mother Theresa had a clear life mission to help the poor of India. A government clerk named Albert Einstein had a mission to correct humankind's understanding of the universe. Princess Diana had a clear life mission to ban the use of land mines. One of the life missions of U.S. President Abraham Lincoln was to eliminate slavery. One of the life missions of British Prime Minister Sir Winston Churchill was to prevent Nazism from conquering England and the world. Shakespeare's life mission was to present the rich diversity of human emotions and experience through the written English word.

These are examples from some of the most famous figures of history. Your life mission may be more humble than theirs. But your own life mission is nevertheless lofty for you. It is an uplifting and inspirational overview of your life. For example, your life mission may be to be a great parent, to be a loving spouse, to help disadvantaged children, to help the ill, to entertain, to be a model of integrity, and so on.

One of my own life missions is to educate. I have dedicated my life to teaching principles that really work, and to helping my clients significantly increase their wealth and other aspects of their quality of life. This book is one way I am fulfilling my own life mission.

Another way I am fulfilling this life mission of teaching is by offering The Monthly Mentor program. Each year we do the My Life Missions™ exercise. It is one of the highlights of the year. Monthly Mentor members talk about being able to see their own life as a whole. They talk about being able to see their life as a *product* that they can refine and improve and work on. What a great advantage.

If I can revise Michael Gerber's famous quotation to make it relevant to this chapter: *Don't just work in your life; work on your life!*

Basically, I am asking you to have an overview of your life, in order to ensure that you get to where you wish to go.

In the Annual Love Letters, you learned that your loves are where you *come from*. In this chapter, you will learn that your life mission is where you are *going to*. Always come from your loves and always aim toward your life mission. With that rule in mind, you will have a deeply fulfilling life of joy *every day* (because you are involved only in your loves) and a deeply fulfilling life *overall* (because you will be achieving what you truly desire to accomplish in this lifetime).

You Have Life Missions

Notice that you are not being asked to *create* a life mission. You already have one or more life missions. You may, at this moment, be unaware of exactly what they are. This chapter will reveal your life missions to you

"The whole life of man is but a point of time; let us enjoy it, therefore, while it lasts, and not spend it with no purpose."

—Plutarch

very clearly. They are already inside you. This chapter simply makes them consciously available to you.

There are three purposes for having a clear statement of your life mission:

1. To focus your attention on what is truly important to you in your life
2. To focus your attention on what to do this year so that you spend this year working toward your life mission
3. To focus your attention on what to do this month so that you spend this month doing those things that may move you toward your life mission

If you do not know your life mission right now, an important question is, *Do I have a life mission?* Yes. First let's seek *spiritual* proof.

Every religion on earth seeks to help you answer three questions:

1. Where did you come from?
2. Why are you here?
3. Where are you going afterward?

The purpose of this chapter is to address the second question. It is the underlying assumption of all world religions that you indeed do have a reason for being here.

Now let's seek *practical* proof that you do have a life mission. My own direct experience that you do indeed have a reason for being here comes from mentoring thousands of clients for decades. Whether they approach this exercise with skepticism or eagerness, they *always* uncover their own life missions. You may have spent considerable time thinking about this topic. My experience, though, is that most people have not. It is an important issue, but, unfortunately, you might be so caught up in the daily tasks of life that such an overview of your whole life might escape you. You will find great value in doing the My Life Missions exercise.

Now that you have some assurance that you have a life mission, the next question is: *How many life missions do I have?* I can answer from my own experience and from the experiences of thousands of eager goal-achievers whom I have mentored over the last two decades. I have noticed that we humans are too complex for simply one life mission. However, we are also unable to handle a dozen life missions—nowhere near that many. The number that has arisen in my work is *three*.

> *"Everyone has his own specific vocation or mission in life; everyone must carry out a concrete assignment that demands fulfillment. Therein he cannot be replaced, nor can his life be repeated, thus everyone's task is unique as his specific opportunity."*
> —Viktor Frankl

Raymond's Life Missions

I am clear on my own life missions. I know what my life is about. It took me a long time to figure this out, but I have now come to know my three life missions. This is what I want in my eulogy. This is what I want on my tombstone. This is what my life is about:

- Great Teacher
- Great Husband
- Great Father

I am not Churchill or Lincoln or Gandhi or any other great world leader. I do not have their historically significant life missions. But, I do have these missions. And, for me, they are lofty. No matter how much money I accumulate, no matter how much I donate to charity, no matter how many athletic achievements I attain—if I have not earned the right to be remembered in these three ways, I will not have done what I came here to do. I will smile in the late December of my life if I am acknowledged by my clients as a Great Teacher, by my wife as a Great Husband, and by my children as a Great Father. That's what I'm aiming for. That will determine the quality of my life.

How have I done? The truth is that I am a work in progress like you are. Luckily, I have time to continue working on my three life missions. I am not yet where I wish to be in these three categories. I have work to do; you do, too. We all do.

I am deeply loved by my two daughters, Juli-Ann and Emma, and by my two step-daughters, Lori and Lisa. If I died today, "Great Dad" would be in my eulogy. And I will continue in this lifetime to earn and re-earn their love.

I am loved and admired by many thousands of my clients around the world. If I died today, "Great Teacher" would be in my eulogy. And I will continue to earn and re-earn their love and respect.

I am, alas, at the moment not married. So "Great Husband" would be missing. Thankfully, I am a work in progress.

Uncovering Your Life Missions

Let's begin the fascinating and revealing journey to identify *your* three life missions.

Think about how you wish to be remembered. In other words, what key points would you like spoken at your eulogy? What key points would you want (metaphorically, not literally) engraved on your tombstone?

This tombstone question is metaphorical. You may not actually want your mission physically engraved on your headstone. However, remember the case of Roger Maris. His life mission was to be a great baseball player. In 1961, he broke Babe Ruth's record of 60 home runs in a single season. Proudly engraved on Roger Maris's tombstone is the brief epitaph, "61 in 61."

Let's get you started. Your first step is to have in front of you a special form called *My Life Missions* (see Figure 3.1). You can obtain a copy of this form in two ways:

- Photocopy the form from this chapter. Unfortunately, due to the size of the pages of this book, the form is presented smaller than normal.
- Download a full-size, full-color, printer-friendly version of this form from www.aaron.com/DoubleYourIncome.

Personalize your form by neatly printing your name *twice*: once at the top and once in the tombstone. Next, enter today's date, including the year.

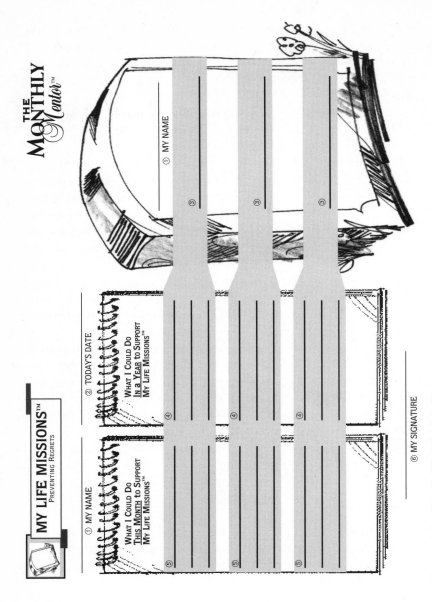

Figure 3.1   Blank Life Mission Form

Sit quietly. Think of your whole life and begin to identify what is truly important to you in your life. Think of how you wish to be remembered. Think of what would make you proudest to hear about yourself. Think of the loftiest desire you have in this lifetime. Record this as your first life mission.

Humans are multifaceted and complex creatures. We are multi-dimensional. Taking this into account, it certainly seems reasonable that you would have more than one life mission. In mentoring thousands of clients over the years, I have come to realize that you have *three* major life missions that comprise your overall purpose for being here. So, with that in mind, redo the same exercise and identify two more life missions. (See Figure 3.2 for a completed form.)

It is more important to record three *possible* life missions than to write nothing. This is a *process*. You may record all three and they may indeed be the most accurate depiction of your life. On the other hand, over the years, you may notice that your life mission changes as you clarify your vision or as your life changes. So, be brave and record the three *best* life missions you can determine at this time.

Focus now on your *first* life mission. Are you at a place in your life where you have already achieved it? Has that particular achievement already earned its way into a eulogy of your life? In other words, have you already achieved that status and just want to continue doing it and improving, or do you need to do some work to arrive there? In either case, there is work you can do to get better and better at this life mission.

As an example, let's say your first life mission is "Great Dad." What can you do this year to move you toward that life mission? Three specific things you might do this year are:

- Take my son on a fishing trip this summer.
- Help my son to improve in hockey.
- Ensure my son has a wonderful birthday party.

Now it is your turn. Based on your first life mission, record *three* actions you could do this year to support it.

Now you should begin to feel the power of working backwards from your long-term vision to what you could do this year to create it. You know where you're going and you know what to do this year to begin to achieve that glorious vision.

PURPOSE:

- To focus you on what is truly important in your life
- To focus you on what to do this year
- To focus you on what to do this month

BENEFITS:

so that you .... will get what you want this lifetime.
so that you .... will spend the year working toward your Life Missions™.
so that you .... will spend this month working toward your Life Missions™.

Please Follow These INSTRUCTIONS:

A. Neatly print your ① Name **twice**, where shown, both in the header and also in the gravestone. Record ② Today's Date.
③ Think of what is ultimately, truly, and deeply important to you in your life. Record one, two, or three such Life Missions™.
④ For the first Life Mission™, record what you could do **this year** to move closer to that lifetime desire. These are **not** goals, just ideas or suggestions.
⑤ Record what you could do soon to support your yearly desire.
⑥ Sign your name to show your commitment to your life's desires.

LINKS TO OTHER FORMS:

A. Review your recorded ideas of what you could do **this year**. You may wish to convert all or some of them into goals in your Annual Backwards Goals™ (Next Year's Goals, As If Already Achieved) form. Or, you may wish to store them for future consideration in your Future Generator™ (Inventory of Future Achievements), selecting the appropriate Goal Category for each idea.

B. Review the ideas of what you could do **this month**. If you do desire to implement a particular idea immediately, you may wish to record it in this month's MAINLY™ (Measurable Monthly Progress) form, selecting the appropriate Goal Category for it. If you will **not** be immediately implementing a particular idea, you may wish to store it in your Future Generator™ (Inventory of Future Achievements), selecting the appropriate Goal Category.

SAMPLE:

WHAT I COULD DO
THIS MONTH to SUPPORT
MY LIFE MISSIONS™

⑤ Go to the annual Boat Show and buy a boat
Call my son's friend's private hockey coach
Check Yellow Pages for Party ideas

WHAT I COULD DO
IN a YEAR to SUPPORT
MY LIFE MISSIONS™

④ Take my son on a fishing trip this Summer
Help my son improve in hockey
Ensure he has a wonderful Birthday Party

John Smith
① MY NAME

③ Great Dad

Figure 3.2 Completed Life Missions Form

44

What is the next step? The next step is to think of one thing you could do *this month* to support each of the annual tasks. Here are some examples:

- To support getting the fishing trip done this year, you may choose to go to the Boat Show this month to look at boats.
- To help your son to improve in hockey this year, you may choose to call a private hockey coach for kids this month.
- To create a wonderful birthday party for your son this year, you may choose to check Google this month for party ideas.

You are still working on your first life mission and on the three annual goals you just recorded to move you closer to your first life mission. Now record one action you could take this month to support *each* of your three annual goals for this *first* life mission.

"Your life is a product that you can improve."

—Raymond Aaron

Now redo this same procedure for each of your remaining two life missions. Sign the form to commit to your own life.

In The Monthly Mentor, we redo this fascinating process each year. It is always exciting to get feedback from my mentored clients around the world who have redone the My Life Missions process several times. They consistently talk about getting clearer and clearer about what they have chosen to produce in the world.

You will be invited in the Three Expert Action Steps™ of this chapter to complete the My Life Missions exercise. You will find that it changes over time. My clients in The Monthly Mentor program redo this exercise regularly every December and deeply enjoy the insights gained from this annual exercise.

Analyzing Your Life Missions

Take a blank sheet of paper and entitle it, "Insights Gained." Please also date it with the year. Now, record your own insights:

- Think of how easy or difficult it was to identify your life missions.
- Think of how confident you are that these three are your most accurate missions.

- Think of how you can strategically orient your life, based on making decisions consistent with your life missions.
- Think of how you feel knowing that you have a plan for this year and for this month to move you confidently toward your life missions.

Record these insights. They are a statement of where you truly are right now in your own life. Without this introspection, you are doomed to live an uninvestigated life filled with the everyday noises and routines of the daily grind—instead of a life filled with the joy of achieving what you truly wish to achieve.

Using Your Life Missions to Improve Your Life

You've done the work. Now, let's get the benefit.

"How do you know if your mission in life is finished? If you're still alive, it isn't."
        —Richard Bach, author of
        Jonathan Livingston Seagull

Take another blank sheet of paper and entitle it, "Future Actions." Date it. On this sheet of paper you are to record every idea that relates to what you can do to alter your life in ways suggested by your My Life Missions exercise:

- What actions may be missing from your life that you would like to add? How do you intend to do that? And when?
- Are you noticing that your life could be much fuller? Are you noticing that there is something missing? What is it? It is better to find it out now and correct it than be regretful on your deathbed. How can you correct it? And when?
- What has caused you sadness, regret, or feelings of failure while doing this exercise? How do you intend to change that? And when?
- Think of the insights you have gained that give you ideas as to what you can do now to improve your life. How do you intend to do that? And when?

FAQs

1. **How often should I redo this exercise?**
   This exercise (plus the Annual Love Letters) needs to be redone annually. Your life will have changed and your list of loves and

your life missions will change with it. Your priorities change. As you accomplish current goals, bigger goals emerge that may not even be imaginable to you right now. It is those future goals and desires that will be the focus of next year's Annual Love Letters exercise and next year's My Life Missions exercise.

2. **Does everyone have a life mission?**
   Yes, but most people are totally unaware of their own. You are likely not merely here to pay bills and commute to work. As the highest form of creature that has ever evolved, you likely have a bigger purpose than just getting by. In my opinion, it is your sacred duty to discover your own life missions, so that you have heightened meaning in your life.

3. **Why should I work backwards from the lifetime to the annual to the monthly?**
   If you wish to get somewhere, you first need to know where that is. Then you need to ensure that your year is focused on getting there. Finally you need to strategically focus your month toward that annual and lifetime aim. A well-designed life can be envisioned only backwards. Determine where you will end up, and then plan how to get there.

4. **What happens if I cannot clearly identify my life missions?**
   Just do your best. As time goes on, you will change and so your life missions will change. Further, as you ponder this important question over the months and years to come, you will become clearer and clearer and you will therefore be able to record your life missions more accurately. For now, just start the process without worrying about the ultimate correctness.

Three Expert Action Steps

You know you have three life missions. You realize the strategic value in identifying three tasks you could do this *year* to support each one of your three life missions. You see the value in identifying one specific task you could do this *month* to support your annual goal that would thereby also support your life mission. You know great insights are to be gained by doing this exercise.

It is time to use this knowledge. Below are listed the Three Expert Action Steps designed to support you in bringing what you have just read into play in your life.

First Expert Action Step: Complete the exercises suggested in this chapter.

Photocopy the form shown in this chapter or download a full-page, full-color, printer-friendly version of this form from www.aaron.com/LifeMissions. Complete it using the instructions in this chapter as your guide. Then, record your insights as suggested and record your own ideas for action, as also suggested.

Second Expert Action Step: Select one mission you particularly wish to experience more and decide how you will go about implementing that goal.

Likely one of your life missions leaves you with the distinct feeling that you could do much more. Select that one. Instead of just the three annual goals and the three monthly goals suggested in the form, you may wish to record *10* annual tasks plus one monthly goal that supports each one of the corresponding annual goals. This will ensure that you move forward most quickly on the one life mission that you feel needs more attention.

Third Expert Action Step: Make entries in your calendar to ensure you are successful at these tasks.

You may wish to make the following entries in your calendar:
- Make an entry in your calendar to redo this exercise next December.
- Make an entry in your calendar one month from now to check to see how many of the monthly goals you set in the First and Second Expert Action Steps have been accomplished.
- Make an entry in your calendar one year from now to check to see how many of the annual goals you set in the First and Second Expert Action Step have been accomplished.

Moving On

Congratulations. You know where you come from and where you are going to. The next chapter provides you with a tool to help you uncover those *special talents* unique to you.

As a special treat, you may be quite moved to watch a very touching video at www.aaron.com/PersonalVideo, where I will personally reveal to you a sacred connection I had with my daughter Juli-Ann that not only supported my life mission of Great Dad but also set her on a quest to find her special talents, which is the subject of the next chapter.

CHAPTER 4

Your Special Talents

HOW YOU CAN ENJOY THE PLEASURE AND HEIGHTENED INCOME OF FOCUSING YOUR WORKING LIFE PRIMARILY ON YOUR SPECIAL TALENTS

Ancient Egyptian hieroglyphics—it is the most complicated language ever created. It is so very complex that, up till recently, no one was able to decipher it. Imagine, with all the computer power, mathematical skill, and linguistic advances, no one was able to figure out what hieroglyphics meant.

One day, in 1799, an engineer in Napoleon's army was on duty near the Egyptian city of Rosetta (Rashid) on the Nile. He found a very heavy, jet-black polished slab of basalt, one foot thick, two feet wide, and four feet high. There was writing engraved on it. He unearthed it and brought it back to study.

Linguists, Egyptologists, and historians around the world rejoiced. Why? Because this slab, since dubbed the *Rosetta Stone,* contained an edict of a long-dead Pharaoh in *triplicate*—each in a different language. One was hieroglyphics; the other two languages were ones that linguists could already read. Being able to read the same edict twice in the two known languages, they quickly realized that the third part must be the same edict in hieroglyphics. Rejoicing, they deciphered hieroglyphics for the first time ever—because of the Rosetta Stone.

"Rosetta Stone" is now a term applied to a tool or a concept that is the key to understanding something else of great value. The Rosetta Stone was the key to understanding hieroglyphics. It opened up a realm of study and understanding that had previously lain dormant and hidden. It was indeed a special key.

What is the relevance of the Rosetta Stone to goals? There is a special key in goal-setting. There is a Rosetta Stone that can convert what was previously unknown and puzzling into clarity, happiness, and wealth.

What is it, in goal-setting, that is unknown and puzzling? What is puzzling is the question: *What should I be doing today?*

What should you focus your energies on each day? What should you be spending your time doing? Of all the different tasks you could be doing today, which ones are the *best* ones for you to be doing?

You have a clue from the chapter on the Annual Love Letters™, where you learned that you need to come from your loves. You have another clue from the chapter on your Life Missions™, where you learned that you should aim toward your life mission. We created the metaphor that life is a pathway that leads from your loves toward your life missions. This is your life *overview*. This tells you what your life should be about on a year-to-year or decade-to-decade basis.

But, the question of *this* chapter has to do with what to do on a daily and hourly basis. The concepts of the Annual Love Letters and your *life missions* are too grand to be of value when deciding what you should do each hour and each day. For example, if you need to do some yard work at your home or clean the garage, it does not seem worthwhile to review your list of loves or contemplate how you want your eulogy to read, decades hence.

You need another tool. You need another concept. You need a key. You need that Rosetta Stone to crack the code of how you should spend your days and hours. Yes, the question needing a Rosetta Stone is: *How should I spend my day?*

Less Is More

The answer is that you need to identify your *special talents*. And then you need to focus your daily life, as much as possible, on your special talents.

This immediately raises lots of questions. Do you have special talents? Yes, you do! Does everyone have special talents or are some people talented and others not? *Everyone* has special talents. How many special talents do you have? You have anywhere from a half-dozen to a dozen. We will discuss how to identify your own special talents later in this chapter.

The more you focus on your special talents, the more you will realize the joy of having fewer and fewer activities to do in your daily life. This chapter focuses on explaining this concept.

It is easy to do many things as long as you are willing to be mediocre at most things you do. Face it—you do hundreds of activities throughout the year and you are exceptional at only a few of them and competent at a few dozen more. In all the other activities you are merely mediocre or downright incompetent. The more you spend your time doing what you are less-than-brilliant at, the more you will have a life of frustration and lowered income.

Let's use my life as an example. When I was younger, I did many things. Now that I am older and wiser, I do three things—*three*—that is all.

When I first started in business, I did it all. I was the bookkeeper. I hired and trained the staff. I booked the meeting rooms. I organized my own hotel accommodation and rental cars. I paid the bills. I did the annual income tax returns for myself and my company. I even had time left over from all this to give the lectures—which was, at that time, the whole point of the company. I did it all because (in my mind) I was a clever, multitalented guy. And it worked. My business flourished. But, I was exhausted.

It was hard to get good staff. If I wanted something done, I had to do it myself. I was low on vacation time and low on family time.

So, though it seemed to be working, there was some error in the construction of my life's daily duties. And, there were some cracks in the foundation of my daily life.

The error was imagining that, just because I could get a task done, therefore I should be doing that task. The error was focusing on the money I was supposedly saving by doing those tasks myself instead of doing what I loved.

As I began understanding life and business, I came to realize the paradox that *narrowing* my range of permitted duties would give me a *grander* life. Consciously *restricting* myself to doing only a few activities would actually give me *freedom* from this grind.

How Can Narrowing Create a Grander Life? How Can Restricting Give Freedom?

Yes, this does sound paradoxical. But, what you currently believe has *created* your current situation. You, of course, do what you believe. Hence, what you believe *causes* your situation. The age-old saying, *I'll believe it when I see it,* is actually wrong. Strangely, the correct version is the exact opposite: *I'll see it when I believe it.* In other words, it is only what you believe that you produce. You know exactly what you believe—just look around you at what you've got. That is what you believe! This is, of course, the result of the Law of Attraction having been relentlessly working in your life up till now. If you desire a different future, you must *now* have different thoughts and beliefs.

How Do You Break Out of This Mold and Leap Upward to a More Joyous and Higher-Income Life?

The answer to doing more in your life lies in the paradox that you need to do *less.* The answer to how to enjoy more is ironically to do less. It is so contrary to ordinary thinking that it needs a Rosetta Stone to unlock this mystery.

I do not mean you should work less. No; I mean restricting yourself, as much as possible, to doing only certain specific activities in your life.

The Problem with Doing It All

What happens to you when you do everything? There are four major results to this course of action—*all negative.*

You are really *great* at a few activities. You are *good* at many more. You are *mediocre* at practically everything else. Finally, there is even a list of activities that you are downright *terrible* at. This is not a condemnation. This is just a reality. You are human; you have certain abilities; you are not Superman. (Indeed, even Superman had his weakness.)

If you restrict yourself, as much as possible, to doing only those activities in which you excel, you will have a blessed and high-income life. As you expand into those areas of lesser competence, you make more errors and obviously earn less. So, the first negative result of doing it all is that you are spending a certain amount of your time *doing what you are not great at.*

A second problem with doing it all is that you will have lots of *frustration and anxiety* in your life. Why? Because you are spending your time doing those tasks for which you are not highly qualified. You do not love them, so you do not focus your energies at becoming better at them. You do not eagerly read how-to books on them, so you never improve much in them. Hence, you are spending your time at what you neither are good at nor ever will be good at. Frustration arises from realizing that you will never get any better.

A third problem is *procrastination.* You procrastinate on only those tasks that you do not enjoy doing. So, not only is the doing of the task less than exciting for you, but the agonizing preamble to the task is hours or years of not getting around to doing it. The unpleasantness thus lasts for far longer than the mere time to do the task—it extends earlier into the dreaded procrastination stage as well. I will unveil the remedy to this ill in the next chapter, "Curing Procrastination Forever."

The fourth important negative result of doing what you are not particularly good at is that your income is significantly lower than it could be. You will read a fascinating story later in this chapter about a colleague of mine whose income skyrocketed from $60,000 a year to $300,000 a year when he began focusing on his special talents. But first, enjoy a lesson from my own life.

Raymond's Special Talents

I began many years ago shedding from my daily chores those tasks that I was downright terrible at. What a relief; what *liberation.* How did I do it? I hired staff to support me. I formed strategic alliances with colleagues who did certain important functions necessary to the success of my business. I used outside contractors. I rearranged my duties with them, taking from them what I liked and giving to them what they liked.

Did all this cost money? Not really; I did this over time. I brought in new liberating ideas, one at a time. As each chore was removed from my daily life, the liberation allowed me to breathe more deeply and allowed me to enjoy life more fully. *I began to procrastinate less because there was less to procrastinate about.* Whatever I did not enjoy, I got rid of. What a plan! My income began to dramatically rise, so there was really no cost.

As the years progressed, I eliminated more and more duties. I work just as hard now. But, I hardly notice I am working because I love every single moment of every day. Why? Because I am focusing only on my special talents. You can get there, too. But, it is a process over time.

Where am I now? I have now reached a glorious level in my daily life. I have arrived at what I now perceive to be really close to the *special talents summit*. The secret is identifying and then restricting yourself to your special talents.

I no longer do bookkeeping, hire, organize, pay bills, do the taxes, and so forth. I do only *three* activities in my daily working life:

1. I design educational materials.
2. I teach.
3. I inspire individuals to be all that they can be.

That's it; that is what my business day is all about—nothing else. Let me share with you these three activities.

First, I love designing educational materials. I design lessons for The Monthly Mentor™ program every month. I write books. I reply by e-mail to the queries of Monthly Mentor members and answer their questions. I design workshops and seminars to teach different aspects of wealth creation. I am constantly thinking of new ways to teach what I know in different formats and with greater clarity. This goes on all the time, in my mind. I carefully review the educational materials offered by other firms. I take lots of courses and workshops. I am a student of educational materials and I am a creator of educational materials. I open my laptop on airplanes and write a chapter of a book or design the new Monthly Mentor lesson. This is not work—this is *love*.

Second, I love delivering dazzling presentations. I notice what works and what does not work in every speech and make corrections and improvements daily. While on airplanes, I spend hours improving and fine-tuning my PowerPoint presentations on different topics. I listen intently to other great speakers and I notice what works and what does not work so that I can put that wisdom into my own lectures. And, I actually deliver a couple hundred lectures each year. I am a student of public speaking and I am a practitioner of public speaking. I love it.

Third, I love motivating and inspiring others to be all that they can be. When I am speaking with clients, I often alert them to how they are invoking the Law of Attraction badly. I then show them how to rephrase their statement in the positive so that the Universe can deliver to them what they really desire versus what they otherwise would have inadvertently received. They smile; they leave with a glow and a heightened vision for themselves. They love it. I love it.

Those are my three special talents. There are a few other duties I have during my business day that take up no more than a few hours a month. I do sign checks and I do review the monthly statements of my firm. I have no special talent in check-signing or in report-reading, but these are activities that I still do. Maybe, one day, I will let those go, too. Right now, well over 95 percent of my daily activities are my special talents.

You have special talents. You might never have thought of them as special talents. You might not want to boast and hence might be unwilling to puff up your abilities by labeling them as special talents. Nevertheless, you have them. Furthermore, it is your sacred duty to uncover them and devote your time each day to delivering them to the world. Why is that so?

To answer this question, let's look again at my life. I have the special talent of being able to present complicated topics in an easily understandable way. Hence, my clients can achieve what they were unable to achieve before learning from me. They are therefore able to overcome their obstacles and achieve their goals and dreams. I am, in my small way, bettering a bit of the world by enhancing others' abilities and others' successes.

Now, to the contrary, imagine that I took some of that time away. Instead of designing a brilliant new workshop that could help many people achieve their goals and instead of delivering that workshop to my clients, let's say that instead I did the bookkeeping for my company in order to save some money.

Would I really be saving money? No, because I make far more money designing and delivering brilliant workshops than I could ever earn bookkeeping. Furthermore, I am really efficient at designing and delivering workshops but I am really slow and error-prone in bookkeeping because I am not good at it. I might save a few hundred dollars and miss earning many thousands of dollars. I might spend a few days of frustration agonizing my way through the bookkeeping tasks instead of being uplifted with the joy of completing a brand-new workshop. Even more, no one would benefit from my doing the books, whereas thousands of my clients would benefit from a new workshop.

Your Special Talents

Is it easy to identify your special talents? No, it isn't. Why is that so? Because you were misled throughout school. In school you were given homework in every subject. Some subjects you excelled at and some you were mediocre at. Regardless, you had to do your own homework in each subject. If you got some help, you were admitting that you were weak and needed help. If you got a lot of help (in other words, if someone else actually did your homework for you), you were called a *cheater*. So, getting a little help was not macho and getting a lot of help was dishonest. That is the unfortunate and incorrect lesson you were taught day after day throughout school.

> *"If you spend your life improving your weaknesses, at the end of your life you will have many strong weaknesses."*
>
> —Dan Sullivan,
> *The Strategic Coach*™

You are now left with the sense that you should do it all yourself. You are left with the sense that doing it all yourself is somehow good and worthy. I am here to present the other viewpoint, which I feel is far superior.

Here is the four-point thinking process to identify your special talents:

1. Think of what brings you the greatest joy at work.
2. Think of what you always do first, if you have an option.
3. Think of what you make the most money doing—or you would *like* to make the most money doing.
4. Think of what you are most skilled at—or would love to *become* most skilled at.

The first two criteria are clear. What brings you the greatest joy and what do you tend to do first, before other tasks, when you have a choice?

The next two need a little explanation. What do you currently make the most money at or what would you *like* to make the most money at? You may have a love that earns you little or nothing now, but you would surely enjoy having *that* be your way to earn money.

Possibly you are not yet far enough advanced in your career. Possibly you do not yet have sufficient credentials.

What are you most skilled at or what would you love to be most skilled at? Possibly you are just not yet sufficiently skilled at it because you are still learning. Possibly you need to take more courses.

That activity or job function that satisfies those four criteria is your first special talent.

Record it. Maybe you have identified your special talent exactly, maybe not. It does not matter as much as recording *something*.

The reason for that lies within the game of horseshoes. When you throw the horseshoe, it occasionally lands surrounding the iron post. That's called a "ringer." But, even if it lands nearby, you still get points. It is the same with your working life. It is better to spend your working day doing what is *close* to your special talent versus doing whatever happens to happen. It is better to begin to move toward your special talents. You can refine them later. I refined my special talents many times as I got clearer and clearer over the years. Also I have noticed that my Monthly Mentor members keep refining their special talents over a period of years until they get a ringer.

So, as a start, get as close as you can. Maybe you've scored a ringer the first time. Months or years from now you will be able to refine your ideas more clearly and perhaps be able to get an even better ringer.

Now, think again to identify your second special talent. Identify your third special talent. Keep going to identify *between two and five* special talents, because if you find only one and attempt to restrict your working life to doing mostly this one function, your life will be limited. Your working life will seem too narrow and confined. If you identify dozens of duties, you will be working in your areas of weakness for most of them. Select two to five only. I have selected three for myself.

Dramatically Increase Your Annual Income

There are many reasons to restrict yourself to, *as much as possible*, only your special talents. They include feeling happier and more fulfilled, providing a greater service to humankind, ending procrastination forever, and dramatically increasing your income.

Let's now discuss the interesting topic of how you could increase your income by focusing on your special talents.

Frank Sinatra could have ushered patrons to their seats. He was a gentleman and would have been great at it. Patrons would have loved it. He could have collected tickets at the door. He could have rented the music halls to save some money by eliminating the booking agents. He could have made

"Frank Sinatra didn't move pianos."
—Dan Sullivan,
The Strategic Coach

his own travel arrangements. He could have tuned his own piano—he did, after all, have perfect pitch. And, with some help and if the piano had been on rollers, he could have moved that piano, too.

It seems that he could have saved lots of money by doing many of the tasks that he chose to pay others to do. But, we know that this is silly. Not because Mr. Sinatra was too wealthy to move pianos, but because you realize that his income would have *dropped* if he had tried to save money by doing all these other tasks. It would be a false economy. It would be a waste of his special talent. It would tire him out. It would dilute his focus. It would detract from his aim in life. It would water down his life mission. He would have had less time and less energy and less focus to deliver his special talent of singing to the world.

But that example was of a wealthy and famous man. Possibly you are now thinking that only such people have special talents. So, let's focus on a more everyday example. This is the example I promised to tell you about earlier in this chapter.

Let me introduce you to a friend of mine, Jason. He was the top salesman for a small service company. How did this company sell? A salesman would make cold calls to book appointments. That salesman would then deliver his one-hour presentation to the prospect, in a meeting room in the office. If the sale was made, the salesman completed the paperwork. If the sale was not made, the salesman would call that prospect back at a later date and attempt to rebook an appointment and make the presentation again, which often worked to make the sale.

One day the company was sold, much to the surprise of the staff. A new president was brought in to take over. The new president's first order of business was to interview each staff member. At the end of that process, having gotten to know each one, the president called a meeting to make a startling announcement. He declared that each staff member was *allowed to do only their special talents*. The staff looked around at each other quizzically.

Jason loved selling, but hated cold-calling and hated re-calling those whom he failed to close the first time. He disliked booking appointments and always procrastinated in doing the paperwork. Of course, he previously had to do all those tasks because they were simply part of the job. How could he complain? He was, after all, top salesman of the company, year after year. He earned $60,000 and he knew that was good because he was the best the company had ever had.

The president calculated that Jason spent 15 percent of his time in front of highly qualified prospects and wearily spent the rest of his working day doing other tasks. The highest and best use of Jason's time was selling. He loved it and he was great at it. The new president reorganized the job description of every staff member, giving Jason the task of making presentations to highly qualified new prospects for one hour each, at 9 A.M., 10 A.M., 11 A.M., 1 P.M., 2 P.M., and 3 P.M.—that was all. Then he had to go home early every day!

Jason scoffed at the absurdity. Where would these prospects come from? The president said that they would come from the cold-calling that other staff members who hated selling yet loved cold-calling would do. Jason was shocked. Were there such people? Yes; and there were those who loved paperwork but not selling or cold-calling. And there were those who hated cold-calling but loved calling back those who had already had a presentation, to attempt to rebook them.

The new plan was implemented. The staff was intrigued, but mostly skeptical and hesitant. What happened? The result startled everyone—except the president. He was not surprised because he knew the truth about special talents. The profitability of the company skyrocketed. The productivity of each staff member skyrocketed. The happiness level of the whole staff skyrocketed. The illness and absenteeism levels plummeted. And what of our friend, Jason? His income leaped from $60,000 a year to $300,000 a year in one month!

How was this possible? He did not take a sales course. He did not work longer hours. Indeed, he worked fewer hours! He did not come in on weekends, because no appointments were booked for him on weekends. The startling explanation is that he was always earning $300,000 a year, year after year. At least, he was earning *at the rate of* $300,000 a year for the 15 percent of his daily work life when he was delivering his one-hour sales presentation in front of highly qualified prospects. The rest of his time was spent doing work that was worth about $15,000 a year. Why was it so low? Because he was not good at it. He procrastinated. He took lots of coffee breaks doing those other tasks. He got ill occasionally.

When you earn $300,000 a year restricted to a small portion of your week and then earn a minimal wage for the majority of your work week and then add to the mix lengthy breaks and illnesses, you arrive at $60,000.

That is the shocking truth for you, too. There are special activities you do that, if you could do just those activities all day long, would earn you many times more than you currently earn. You may find this hard to believe; so did I; so did my friend, Jason; but we found out it was true. You will too. Just begin the journey.

To the extent that you do activities that are not your special talents, you are a $300,000-a-year-income person whose paycheck shows only $60,000!

Your earning power dramatically rises when you do more and more of what meets the four criteria listed previously. It takes time. It takes concentration. It takes courage. It takes educating others around you. But the rewards are significantly heightened income, and less illness, because you are so happy at work. You will have more joy in the workplace and there will be less cause for procrastination.

Rosetta Stone Revisited

The key to unlocking the mystery of what you should do with your daily life is your two-to-five special talents. Remember that these special talents are not necessarily earth shaking and momentous activities. If you are in sales, then meeting prospects and clients needs to be a larger and larger part of your day, because you are good at it. If you are very detailed and accurate, then spend as much of your day as possible doing detail work that rewards high levels of accuracy.

You now have a pathway. It comes from your loves. It goes to your life missions. And it gets narrower and narrower as you define your special talents more clearly and commit more fully to spending your days doing mostly your special talents. The narrower your path, the happier you will be and the wealthier you will become.

The Rosetta Stone that unlocked the mystery is your special talents. Uncover them; nurture them; hone them; cherish them; improve them. And, most important, spend your days doing them—and as little else as possible.

FAQs

1. **What should I do if I am an employee and cannot rearrange my own duties?**
   Have you tried? Many of my mentored clients are employees and have succeeded in dramatically changing their work environment. They approach their boss with a clear plan. For example: "I do not do this task well, but Jessica does. Jessica does not do that task well, but I'd love to and I'm rather good at it. I propose we switch, and Jessica likes the idea." It is tough for a boss to nix a clear proposal that makes his company more efficient and his staff more productive. Be creative. Be courageous. It is worth the effort.

2. **What is the difference between loves and special talents?**
   A love is an *experience* you enjoy—possibly being with your family members, traveling, or reading. A special talent is a *skill*. There is overlap, but there is also a difference. Basically, there are loves that may not be special talents. In other words, you may love doing something that you are not particularly skilled at but enjoy. However, in the other direction, I suspect that you would love doing every one of your special talents. For example, I love going to the movies, but I have no special talent in that regard. And I love riding my unicycle, but I am definitely not that good at it.

3. **How long might it take to convert my working life to doing only my special talents?**
   That answer is different for each person. It depends on how clearly you identify your special talents and on how dedicated you are to moving forward persistently toward doing only those special talents.

4. **What should I do if I am unsure what my special talents are?**
   You will be relieved to know that I have an answer that has helped many Monthly Mentor members over the years. Simply select 10 people who know you well and send them the following e-mail:

   Dear Juli-Ann:
   You know me well, indeed so well that in some ways you may know me better than I know myself. I am reading a book that

instructs me to ask a friend to help me, and I am hoping that
you would be that friend. Would you please take a few minutes
to e-mail me back a list of about 10 special talents that you see
that I have? I would greatly appreciate your input and support.

After several friends have replied, use their input to create a
single list of your own special talents. It's a fun and enlightening
exercise.

Three Expert Action Steps

You know the Rosetta Stone secret to answering the question of
how you should spend your days and hours. You know you need to
identify your special talents and then begin the courageous journey
of dedicating your working life to doing, as much as possible, only
those special talents. You know that the benefit to restricting yourself
to doing only your special talents is a life of true joy.

It is time to use what you have learned. Below are listed the Three
Expert Action Steps™ designed to support you in bringing what you
have just read into play in your life. Once you have completed these
Three Expert Action Steps, you will eliminate procrastination from
your life forever, as explained in the next chapter.

> **First Expert Action Step: Identify two to five special talents.**
> Review the four criteria listed in this chapter. Think of what
> you love doing. Think of what you eagerly do first, if you have
> a choice. Think of what would make your workplace a joy if
> that were all you had to do. Also, e-mail 10 friends for help,
> as explained in the FAQs. Record these special talents.

> **Second Expert Action Step: Make a plan to increase the amount
> of time you spend doing one of your special talents.**
> Select one special talent to begin working on. Then list 10 ways
> that you could reorganize your workplace to do more of that
> one special talent even if you are unsure you could succeed in
> such reorganization. Reread this chapter for the many exam-
> ples and suggestions of ideas as to how you could implement
> this yourself in your workplace.

> **Third Expert Action Step: Make entries in your calendar three
> months from now to review your progress and embark on
> this same journey for your next special talent.**

Make an entry in your calendar that will be the date you review your progress. On that future date, review the 10 ways that you had originally imagined would increase the amount of time you spend doing that first special talent. How well have you done? What successes have you enjoyed? How do you feel? Do you have any new ideas as to what other ways might work to increase your time doing that first special talent? Select the next special talent to work on and redo this process.

Moving On

Congratulations! You know where you come from (your loves). You know where you are going (your life missions). And, you know that the pathway from one to the other is narrowed by doing only your special talents.

I hope you enjoyed my video, offered in the previous chapter, revealing how I passed on to my daughter the sacred task of identifying her special talents. Now that you have a deeper understanding of special talents, you may wish to watch that brief video again at www .aaron.com/DoubleYourIncome. I think it will inspire you.

The next piece of the puzzle, explained in Chapter 5, is to take this newfound knowledge and finally eliminate procrastination from your life.

Curing Procrastination Forever

HOW YOU CAN ELIMINATE PROCRASTINATION ONCE AND FOR ALL

Procrastination is about to leave your life forever.

You hate procrastinating; everyone does. Yet, you still do it. At least up till now you have continued to do it, even though you wanted to stop. This chapter reveals the causes of procrastination—and the cure—so that dreaded procrastination will truly leave your life forever. Does that sound wonderful? It truly is.

Two Types of Procrastination

Let us begin the process of understanding procrastination so that you have the wisdom needed to eliminate it. You have procrastinated, at least to some extent, and possibly to a large extent. You are not alone. Twenty percent of North Americans qualify as *chronic* procrastinators. These are individuals who procrastinate so regularly that their work, finances, or personal relationships suffer because of it.

There are two types of procrastinators: optimistic and pessimistic. I will explain both types so that you can determine which kind you are.

If you are an *optimistic procrastinator*, you will be surprisingly optimistic about your ability to complete a task by a specific deadline. You will typically assure yourself that everything is under control; therefore, there is no need to start yet. You may estimate that your project will take only a short time to complete and that there is plenty of time. Reassured by this false sense of security, time passes. You may typically say, "I'll feel more like doing this tomorrow," or, "This isn't a high priority right now."

However, as the deadline fast approaches, you experience the moment of realization, and say to yourself: "I've left it too long. There's not enough time!" Suddenly, you rise to the occasion and exert every effort toward completing the task and, thankfully, your work rapidly progresses. At this point, you may use statements to justify your actions such as, "I do my best work at the last minute," or "I work well under pressure." Ramping it up, the job gets done. There is no other option at this point but to do what needs to get done. Does this sound familiar?

If you are a *pessimistic procrastinator*, on the other hand, you sense right from the start that there is no way that the job will get done. You have that horrid feeling in your gut that this is yet another one of those to-do items that will get simply rewritten into tomorrow's to-do list and then the next day's, over and over again, and really never get done. You will typically blame someone else, saying: "Well, I never really wanted to do it in the first place; I just reluctantly agreed to keep the peace or to appease my boss or my spouse." You use the excuse that you never really intended to do it, or that others should have known that this is the kind of task that you wouldn't actually get done. You may not have the skills required to do it. You may not have the tools to do it. You may have low self-esteem about your ability to competently get the job done.

Which brand of procrastinator are you? Choose one. You are either the optimistic procrastinator or the pessimistic procrastinator. There is actually one other option: You may be one type for certain tasks and the other type for other tasks. I'm very impressed if you fit into this ambidextrous brand. You have achieved supreme status. You can procrastinate in both ways.

Why should you care which type you are? Because the more you understand a problem, the better you can conquer it. Now, let's move on to contemplate on the universality of the problem.

It's an Epidemic

"I'm going to stop putting things off, starting tomorrow."

—Sam Levenson

Why is it that we learn lessons in so many different areas of our life, yet almost no one learns their lesson on procrastination?

This is a gigantic issue. I challenge you to think of any other area of life that is done so poorly. Here are some examples:

- One-third of adult North Americans are so overweight they are defined as obese. That means two-thirds are not obese.
- Two-thirds of North Americans do insufficient exercise. That means one-third of the population exercises sufficiently.
- Twenty percent of North Americans still smoke. That means that 80 percent of North Americans do not smoke.

But procrastination is universal: 100 percent procrastinate and practically 0 percent do not. Why is this so? The answer is that all the other ills, like smoking, overeating, and not exercising, are the ills themselves. Procrastination is thought of incorrectly as the ill, but it is not. When you try to cure the ill of eating trans fats, what you do is you stop eating fried foods and you've solved it. That is the ill itself. You are actually looking at the cause, accurately and correctly. But, procrastination isn't the ill. It isn't the cause. It isn't the problem.

What is the real problem? Here is the crux of the entire chapter. The problem is this: *You are attempting to do what you do not love.*

Think about it. Think of a task which you have recently procrastinated. Maybe it was:

- Complete a project.
- Study.
- Exercise.
- Clean the closet.
- Clean the garage.
- Clean the basement.
- Lose weight.
- Do the taxes.
- Organize your workspace.
- File piled-up paperwork.
- Complete the household chores.
- Make sales calls.
- Follow up on leads.
- Review your finances.
- Write a will.
- Start your Christmas shopping.

Do any of these sound familiar as typically procrastinated tasks in your life?

Where Procrastination Lives

Procrastination lives in the area of your life called "You don't love it

> *"Procrastination is the bad habit of putting off until the day after tomorrow what should have been done the day before yesterday."*
>
> —Napoleon Hill

and yet you try to do it yourself." This is the *only place* where procrastination lives.

If you don't love it and delegate it, it gets done. If you do love and do it yourself, it gets done. If you do love it and yet you delegate it anyway, maybe because you are busy, then it gets done. Procrastination lives in the area of "You don't love it and you try to do it yourself." See Table 5.1.

Delegation and doing what you love *eliminate* procrastination.

Procrastination Is Actually Good

I know it sounds counterintuitive, but stay with me.

Think of one task that you do not want to do, and, it is certain, you do not love it. You may not be competent at it. You may not have the tools to do it. Then, your self-defense mechanism kicks in so that you do not do it. This is actually the *correct* approach. I believe you should do only what you love. Therefore, if there is a task that you need done and you don't love doing it, the correct approach is to *not* do it.

When you stop at not doing it, and therefore it doesn't get done, it is called by the negative word: *procrastination.* If you don't do it, but instead of stopping at not doing it, you go to the correct next step of finding the guidance you need to have it done by others or with others, then it gets done. The ill is not the procrastination.

Procrastination is the self-defense mechanism that correctly keeps you from doing something that you shouldn't be doing in your life, because you are incompetent at it or can't stand doing it or don't like it or whatever.

Table 5.1   Where Procrastination Lives

	Delegation	No Delegation
Love it		
Don't love it		This is where procrastination lives.

The cure for procrastination is to notice that procrastination is the *effect* and not the *cause*. You can't cure an effect.

Let's explore an example. If somebody punches you in the arm, you will get a bruise. If you incorrectly assume that the bruise is the ill, then you

> *"Never put off till tomorrow, what you can do the day after tomorrow."*
>
> —Mark Twain

will try to cure the bruise. But, you know that it is silly to cure a bruise. How do you cure a bruise? If you go to a rough pub and get punched every Friday night, then every Saturday morning you will have a bruise. The wrong approach is to attempt to cure your Saturday morning bruises; it will never happen. This example makes it very clear. The cure is to choose to not go to the pub, so that you do not get punched.

Similarly, the cure for procrastination is to choose to not do that which you do not love, that which you do not have the tools for, or that which you are not good at. The cure is getting help, delegating, teamwork—having somebody do all or part of it *for* you or *with* you.

When you obey the concept that you should do only what you love, then you would never even attempt to accomplish a "to-do" item that requires you to do what you do not love. As soon as you seek other ways to get done what you do not love, you will have cured procrastination forever, without any effort.

If nobody punches you in the arm on Friday night, you don't have to worry about Saturday morning bruises. They won't even occur. You won't have to cure the bruises. They just won't exist any longer.

Procrastination lowers your self-esteem, makes you feel foolish, and lowers your reputation in the eyes of others. Don't try to solve or cure procrastination, per se. Rather, solve the *cause* of procrastination, which is trying to do what you do not love. The way you do that is delegation.

I procrastinate in nothing, because I do only what I love. No one in my office procrastinates because they do only what they love. Interestingly, you personally never procrastinate, either—at least you never procrastinate in those tasks you love to do.

When one of my staff tells me that they do not love a certain task, that task is taken away from them and they are not allowed to do it. The task will be offered to another staffperson; or it will get done by an outside contractor; or we will hire another staffperson; or we will reorganize our business so that that task is no longer needed.

I will not allow any staff member to have any aspect of their work duties that includes something they do not like doing. If I required my staff to do what they do not love, they would procrastinate and my company would suffer.

When I am giving lectures, I will often say, "Put up your hand if there is any part of your job you do not love doing." A forest of hands instantly rises. How sad that everyone performs tasks they do not love. How sad that they instantly know what those tasks are. How sad that employers cannot understand the basic concept that they are impairing their own company by requiring staff to do what they do not love, and therefore reducing productivity and the bottom line.

My dear friend, Martin Rutte, is the co-author of *Chicken Soup for the Soul at Work* (1996, Health Communications Inc.) and is the leading expert in the world on the topic of spirituality in the workplace. In his new book, *Project: Heaven on Earth,* he asks people around the world for their vision of what heaven on earth would be. My answer was: "Everyone on earth doing only what they love." Isn't that a wonderful vision? What a magnificent world that would be.

Procrastination Is Your Mind's Immune System

In what sense is procrastination good? It is your mind's *immune system*! Think of the analogy of the immune system of your body.

When you get a sliver in your finger, your body instantly recognizes this as foreign matter and begins working immediately to remove it. Your body knows what is "you" and what is "not you." It is wonderful programming, without which you would not survive— biologically.

Similarly, your *mind* has an immune system. And, your mind's immune system does the same job as your body's immune system: It instantly recognizes what is "you" and what is "not you." When you record a goal or a to-do item that is not you, your body immediately begins its immune reaction: It sends you messages that you dislike that job; that you will likely never get it done. It is wonderful programming, without which you would wither—emotionally.

When you attempt continually to do what you do not love, you slowly and inexorably die emotionally. You have lower and lower self-esteem. Your reputation drops. Your ability to perform and succeed withers away. What a sad way to construct a life.

Practical Steps to Eliminating Procrastination

How can you personally end procrastination forever in your own life? This is not a theoretical question. You are about to learn a step-by-step practical method for totally eliminating procrastination.

Identify tasks you tend to procrastinate, at home and at work:

- Is it cleaning your car?
- Is it tidying your desk?
- Is it fixing the small items around your home that need attention?
- Is it getting paperwork completed?

There may well be many such tasks. Record as many as you can think of, certainly 10 or more.

These unpleasant duties are the ones that definitely do not belong in your life. You are not good at them. You don't like them. You don't do them well. Others can do these tasks with ease and more skillfully.

Each month, in The Monthly Mentor™ Program, members eliminate from their life dreaded chores they do not love and add to their life exciting items that they do love. As the months roll on, more of what they usually procrastinate evaporates and more of what they rush eagerly and lovingly to do gets added.

I see with pride my Monthly Mentor members attaining this exalted level and it is a great blessing to them and to me.

If that sounds wonderful to you, and you want more details on how you can be mentored by me on getting to this place in your life, simply go to www.aaron.com/EndProcrastination.

You cannot get there from here. It is not one step. It is a *process.* You need to embark on this process and be committed to moving forward, away from things in which you procrastinate and toward doing what you love—each month. The magnificent end result is a life of joy beyond your imagination.

Let me give you an example from my home life so that you can see that this applies in all areas of your life.

For a while, I lived with my teenage daughter. Her neatness level was lower than mine (much lower). The kitchen would be messy after she created even the smallest meal. Constantly I lectured her to clean up after herself. She usually did not. One day I tried reverse psychology.

I told her that I did not want her to ever clean the kitchen. She eagerly accepted. So, that didn't work.

Interestingly, I happen to love cleaning kitchens. I really love the sense of neatness and orderliness that I can create. But, I did not like the feeling of constantly cleaning up after her. It just did not seem right.

Then I suddenly realized that I was violating my own rule that people around me should do only what they love. I asked my daughter, Juli-Ann, one day what home chore she would love to do if I cleaned the kitchen. Immediately she volunteered to do the laundry for both of us. It worked—I was happy to clean the kitchen because she did my laundry. She never put off doing the laundry because she loved it. I never procrastinated in cleaning the kitchen because I loved it. The problem was solved: I delegated my laundry; she delegated cleaning the kitchen. We were both happy. The home was clean without effort.

> *"Procrastination is the art of keeping up with yesterday."*
> —Don Marquis

When you give away those tasks that you don't love or are not good at, you will be happier with the tasks you are left doing. You'll end up looking forward to your schedule. Procrastination will disappear from your life. You never see people procrastinating in doing things they can't wait to work on and that are energizing.

FAQs

1. **What about studying? I'm the only one who can do this.**
   That's not true—delegation does not mean that someone else does it all for you. Delegation means that someone, or some company, or some web site, or some service, does all *or part of it for you* or *with you.* Is there someone who could help you learn? Is there a fellow student who could sit at the same table and do homework or study at the same time as you—to keep you focused on your work or to help you get started? Once you begin thinking of ways that others could do all or part of the job for you or with you, then it is easy to think of ways to get help. That means, to achieve delegation.

2. **I am unable to delegate. I don't think this applies to me.**
   There are many creative ways to delegate. You can delegate to a person, or a company, or a product, or a service:

- When you order a pizza, you have delegated food preparation and food delivery to a company.
- When you use income tax preparation software to do your annual income taxes, the program is doing some or all of the work for you. You have delegated some or all of the work to a computer program or a web site.
- When you leave your car at a dealership to fix some problems, you are delegating auto repair to a mechanic.
- When you hop into a taxi, you are delegating transportation.
- When you ask a neighbor for help fixing something in your home, you are delegating handyman duties.
- When your neighbor's son cuts your grass, you are delegating gardening chores.
- When you ask your spouse to remind you each morning to do your sit-ups, you are delegating "getting started."

Actually, you delegate all the time; you just *imagine* that you don't.

The person you are delegating to will also receive a benefit. That person may love doing a task that you hate doing. That person may be getting paid. She may be getting exposure to new experiences that on her own she would not have the opportunity to be involved in. There are many people who simply enjoy helping others. You may hesitate to ask for help, but remember that people typically love to be asked. So, don't be shy.

3. **I can't afford to delegate.**
Delegating doesn't always come at a price—it can be free! Some ways it can be free are:

- Barter: "I'll prepare your taxes if you fix my car."
- Ask a friend or family member to help; they are often eager.
- Ask one of your employees, if you have them. You are already paying him; why not ask him to do this extra thing for you?
- Ask someone, like a housekeeper or a babysitter, who already works for you and is already in your home. She may be able to simply include this new task in her duties.

Actually paying someone might sometimes save you money in the end. If you're doing something badly and you botch it, you've wasted your time (and money) and you still have to get it done. By delegating it you get it handled right the first time; plus, you're now free to pursue other profit-making endeavors.

I have included many other ways to delegate at www.aaron .com/DoubleYourIncome.

Three Expert Action Steps

In this chapter, you learned that procrastination is not the ill. It isn't the cause or the problem. The problem is that you're trying to do what you do not love. And you learned about delegation.

It is time to use what you have learned. Below are listed the Three Expert Action Steps™ designed to support you in bringing what you have just read into play in your life. Once you have completed these Three Expert Action Steps, you will be ready to move on to the next chapter and stride forward confidently in each of the *six pathways of life*, every month.

> **First Expert Action Step: Choose a task to eliminate from your life through delegation.**
> Make a list of at least 10 tasks, from home or from work, that you do not love and which you typically procrastinate. From that list, select the one task that you perceive would be the easiest to eliminate from your life.

> **Second Expert Action Step: Find a suitable delegation.**
> - Think of an actual person (like Bill or Mary) who could do all or part of that task with you or for you.
> - Alternatively, think of a *type* of person (like a handyman, bookkeeper, housekeeper, neighbor boy, etc.) who could do all or part of it with you or for you.
> - Think of a computer program or a web site that could do all or part of the job for you.
> - Think of a company that could do all or part of it with you or for you.

Eventually you will realize that there are many choices for finding people, companies, services, web sites, and so on, that could do all or part of the task with you or for you.

Third Expert Action Step: Eliminate procrastination.

Contact the person or company or service you identified in the Second Expert Action Step and ask them to do all or part of the task you selected in the First Expert Action Step with you or for you. Do whatever follow-up is needed to ensure that they get the job done. (Interestingly, this is not usually needed because the person you retain is actually better at doing it than you are, so it is ironic that you—the person who can't get the job done—should be in charge of the person who is competent. Nevertheless, it is prudent to watch over the task in an appropriate way to ensure its completion.)

Your work does not stop here. Your next task is to select another task you do not like and delegate that one. In The Monthly Mentor Program, which you can learn about at www .aaron.com/DoubleYourIncome, I mentor you to ensure that you are moving closer to what you love in *six ways each month,* hence ending procrastination.

Moving On

Now that you have learned how to cure procrastination forever, it is time to learn how to live a holistic and balanced life.

6

The Six MAINLY Pathways of Life

HOW YOU CAN CREATE THE RICHEST AND FULLEST POSSIBLE LIFE

There are six pathways of life. For a full and rich life, it is necessary to stride forward confidently in each one of these six pathways, every month.

What is a pathway? It is a major life *category* of activities. For example, you may have heard of the division of life into spiritual, family, financial, and health categories. This is quite traditional, but I have found that it is not very helpful.

What happens if you don't know the six pathways, and therefore you do not take a forward step in each one monthly? The answer is that you become narrow and one-dimensional.

A woman can fall victim to becoming one-dimensional when her first child is born by thinking that the *only* pathway of life is to care for her children. Of course, caring for children is important. But it is not the *only* pathway of life. Women who follow this one-dimensional vision of life get into severe difficulty 25 years later, when their children are raised, educated, married, and gone from the nest. Such women then suddenly feel empty and lost. Let's be clear: All mothers may legitimately feel empty when their children leave home. I am not talking about this natural experience. I am talking about the emptiness that arrives when a woman has followed only one path and then that path dries up. She has no hobbies. She has not cultivated other interests. Her business skills are a quarter-century out of date.

Women are not alone in this error. The typical male error is thinking that making money is the only pathway. Men who follow this lonely path tend to become workaholics, tend to lose their marriage, and tend to notice only too late that they have missed the joy of spending lots of time with their children as they were growing up. Of course, earning money is important. What I am talking about here is the error of thinking that earning money is the *only* pathway.

Following one single pathway can lead to a narrow and unfulfilled life.

What are the six MAINLY™ pathways? Be open when you read them because they will be substantially different from what you have ever heard or imagined.

The six MAINLY pathways of life are:

MESS	Choose to clean a Mess each month.
ACKNOWLEDGMENT	Choose to express gratitude each month.
INCREASE IN WEALTH	Choose to improve your financial situation each month.
NEW	Choose to do something new each month.
LEARN	Choose to learn something each month.
YOURSELF	Choose to do something just for yourself each month.

These six pathways form an acronym: *MAINLY*. In my own life and in the lives of my thousands of mentored clients around the world, the six MAINLY pathways of life form the basis of monthly and annual planning.

When you set a goal in each one of these six pathways, and achieve even a Minimum Level™ of success in each one of these six pathways, you find yourself striding confidently forward in your life. You find yourself following a holistic vision. You find yourself improving *synergistically*, with all aspects of your life helping all other aspects. Your life becomes more whole.

It is important to investigate and clearly understand each pathway.

Choose to Clean a Mess Each Month

The first MAINLY goal pathway is cleaning a mess. A *Mess* is any situation in which what is outside of you is not equal to what is inside of you. In other words, it is any situation in which what you've got is not what you really want. It is any *incongruence* in your life. It is any negative, uncomfortable situation, physical thing, relationship, or aspect of your environment that you are *tolerating*.

Messes rob you of vitality. Messes teach you that you cannot handle tasks. Messes laugh at you. Messes make you cringe. Messes make you apologize to others. Messes diminish you. Messes do not merely belittle you; they actually have a major impact on your financial well-being.

Physicists are familiar with the Law of Entropy, which states that *everything tends toward chaos.* In simpler terms, left on its own, a situation will deteriorate into disorder. Things don't line up or get fixed on their own. So, the bad news is that entropy is always working against you. On its own, the world tends toward messes. It is your duty to counteract entropy to keep your environment orderly. You need to work at it all the time, because entropy is working against you all the time.

After more than 20 years of mentoring so many clients, I have noticed a significant correlation: Wealthy people tend to be orderly, while those who struggle have lots of messes. At first I thought that wealthy people just hire others to clean their messes. Upon closer scrutiny (and after looking into my own life), I realized that it is the ones who *first* clean their messes who *then* become wealthy.

In fact, the deepest wisdom I have come to know concerns the close relationship between wealth and messes. It is encapsulated in this one brief sentence:

Each mess is a lock on the gate that keeps abundance out.

Let's investigate this.

When I ask wealthy people about abundance, they say it is everywhere. They claim that they could create wealth at any time and at any place, without conditions. However, when I ask middle-income or low-income people about abundance, they tell me that *now* is just not the time to expect to get abundance. And they have lots of good reasons why. They also tell me that *where* they are is not a good place to create abundance. And they have lots of reasons why.

Wealthy people, even if they lost everything, could create or recreate wealth at any place and at any time. Others have reasons why now is not a good time and here is not a good place.

Who is wiser on the topic of abundance, the wealthy or the others? Of course, it's the wealthy. But, if the wealthy are correct that abundance is everywhere and if you personally do not experience abundance, then what is the reconciliation of these two truths? The answer is profound: *Abundance is everywhere but you lock it out with every mess in your life.*

There are many aspects to abundance. Let's investigate money for a moment. If you do not experience money flowing freely and rapidly into your savings account, begin counting your messes and notice the correlation. The more messes, the more locks on the gate that keep abundance out.

Physical messes are easiest to see and easiest to conquer. Relationship messes are more damaging and also harder to resolve.

Some physical messes that may be plaguing you include those in

- Your car
- Your clothes closet
- Your desktop
- Your desk drawers
- Your files
- Your garage
- Your basement
- Your tools
- Your taxes
- Your paperwork
- Your last will and testament
- Your computer

One of my favorite examples of messes is what I call "mystery keys." Do you have such keys on your keychain? Are there keys you carry with you at all times that you have no idea what they are for? Do you have keys from places you used to live or used to work?

Some keys might not be useless; they might just be rarely used. For example, do you carry with you at all times the keys to the cottage (which are used only a few times a year and could be more properly stored in your home) or the keys to your safety deposit box (which you access once every few years)?

Rid yourself of useless mystery keys. Store those rarely used keys in your desk drawer or your car's glove compartment or wherever else you will be easily able to retrieve them when needed. You will feel a huge relief from this little process. Every mess you eliminate, *no matter how small,* brings relief of enormous proportions.

You may also have messes in some of your personal and business relationships that need to be cleaned up.

Hopefully, you are now keen to have a complete list of your own messes so that you can begin to conquer them. You can simply take a lined blank sheet of paper, entitle it, "Messes I Wish to One Day Clean," and then list all the messes in your life. Because this is so important, I have created a powerful process called The Future Generator™, which you may learn about at www.aaron.com/DoubleYourIncome.

The next chapter presents a technique for prioritizing your messes; but first, let's look at the remaining pathways of life.

Choose to Express Gratitude Each Month

"Is that all there is?"

This is the title line of a famous song by Peggy Lee. She was gorgeous, rich, and famous. She seemed to have everything. But, this heart-wrenching line of her song reveals a sadly different reality. How can someone have so much and yet feel she has so little?

This is not an isolated case. It seems that the richer some people get, the less fulfilled they become. Why is this so? Here is the answer to this perplexing question.

When you spend money, you are consuming money. When you eat a restaurant meal, you are consuming the meal. When you drive a car, you are consuming the car (in the sense that you are using it up). So, all of spending and all of using and all of consuming is depreciation—making less. You may not have thought of it this way before, but follow me. The conclusion is fascinating.

The more money you earn, the more you can afford to spend, and hence, the more you are depreciating what is around you. Of course, you perceive it as *enjoying*, not *depreciating*. You may well be enjoying the restaurant meal or the fancy car or the vacation or the concerts or the clothes. But it is not merely a matter of experiencing joy; the inescapable reality is that you are definitely depreciating the items that you are consuming and attempting to enjoy.

You hope that you will enjoy the process. The emptiness comes from thinking that you should be enjoying this process, but realizing, for some unknown reason, that you are not enjoying it.

The next piece of this puzzle is that life is *balance*. Everything that goes up must come down. You are refreshed in the morning and then tired at night. You are young and then you are old. Trees grow tall and then fall over. The tide is high and then the tide ebbs. This is the inescapable cycle of life.

When you earn so much that you can afford to spend a considerable amount, then you are actively engaged in the process of depreciation. If that is all you do, then you are violating the basic principle of life, that life is balance. If you focus on just one-half of the equation, then your life is out of balance and you will feel unfulfilled and empty.

What is the opposite of *depreciation*? The opposite is *appreciation*.

When you invest in stocks and those stocks go down, the value of your account is said to have depreciated. When the value of the stocks goes up, you have enjoyed appreciation. When your home gets older without proper maintenance, it is said to have depreciated. When your area enjoys a real estate boom, the value of your home is said to have appreciated.

In the English language, that one word *appreciate* is used for two seemingly different purposes: to get larger and to express gratitude.

I claim that when you appreciate—when you express gratitude—you have created the balance for depreciation; that is, you balance consumption.

The way to have a balanced life is to have your gratitude at least balance your consumption. Indeed, it is better to have more gratitude than spending, that is, more appreciation than depreciation.

> *"The cure for a life of emptiness is a life of gratitude."*
>
> —Raymond Aaron

The more you earn and the more you are able to spend, the more you must consciously increase your gratitude in the world.

Now you can understand why wealthy people who are also happy are the ones who donate large amounts to their favorite charities and volunteer as Board Members for nonprofit organizations and give their time as spokespersons for different important causes in the world.

The cure for a life of emptiness is a life of gratitude. Stated differently, emptiness is simply unbalanced depreciation, or consuming without gratitude.

The answer for the wealthy who feel unfulfilled is for them to express their appreciation to the same extent that they are involved in spending (or depreciating).

We have learned that if you spend (or depreciate) without the balance of expressing your gratitude (appreciating), then the consequence will be emptiness. In other words, the Universe will intercede to cause the pain of emptiness because you are out of balance with universal laws.

How Gratitude Increases Income

Let's look at the issue from the other direction. I personally believe that if you dramatically increase your level of gratitude, you will again cause the Universe to intercede to allow your income to dramatically rise to regain balance.

So, if you do not know this law of balance, although you will increase your income and hence increase your ability to spend, without gratitude, you will be robbed of the joy of spending by the feeling of emptiness.

Conversely, if you understand the law of balance, you can consciously increase your level of gratitude to do two things. First, if your income is higher than your gratitude, then increasing your gratitude will produce joy, not emptiness. Second, if your income is lower than your gratitude, then increasing your gratitude will cause your income to rise to balance your level of gratitude.

What a wonderful concept. If you want to consume (depreciate) more and enjoy that process, just increase your gratitude (appreciation).

The second MAINLY pathway of life is *Acknowledgment*. It is through acknowledging others that you express your gratitude for others' contribution to you. It is also how you appreciate. Appreciation can be expressed toward a person, a group of people, or a company.

You could acknowledge

- Your children
- Your child's teacher, tutor, or coach
- Your clients
- Your suppliers
- Your employees
- Your colleagues
- Your team members
- Your mentors

- Your teachers
- Your fellow committee members
- Your family members
- Your friends
- A salesperson or clerk
- A server at your local coffeeshop

To support me in this pathway of acknowledging, I have a large assortment of thank-you cards in my office. I also keep other items needed to do an elegant job of expressing appreciation. I keep stickers (happy faces, rainbows, starbursts, etc.) and pretty postage stamps. Whenever someone is particularly nice to me or serves me in a particularly outstanding way or when someone helps me, I make a note to send them a card. Next time I am in my office, I write the card, use lots of pretty, colorful stickers, add an attractive postage stamp, and think happy thoughts as I place the sealed envelope in the mail.

Sometimes I get no feedback from the recipient. That's okay; I know it had a wonderful impact on them and I know for sure that it had a wonderful impact on me.

Sometimes, though, I am dazzled by the response. Often they call me to tell me that in their many years on this job, mine was the first thank-you card they had ever received. Sometimes I will be visiting a client's office for the first time and notice a thank-you card on their desk that I had mailed to them many years before.

There is so little formal acknowledgment in the world these days that whatever you do, no matter how little, will make a huge impact.

Since it is the impact that is the point here, my humble suggestion is to not use e-mail or the telephone. These channels are just too commonplace and too easy. Write a personal letter, or send a thoughtful card. You may even want to be outrageous and write a poem. Make it special. The effort will be hugely rewarded.

Let's think of birthdays for a moment. Have you ever been invited to a birthday party? Certainly; but don't be too surprised to learn that, roughly a year later, that same person had another birthday. I can assure you that he knows it is his birthday and it all too often happens that you do not recall it. Of all the billions of people on the planet, you were in the top dozen or so who were special enough to be invited to his birthday party. Then, a year later, you had no recollection whatsoever that it was his special day. That is certainly no way to acknowledge.

An Interesting Example

I keep a record of the birthdays of people important to me and I make a note on my calendar *one week in advance of their birthday* so that I can remember in time to send them a nice card or call them or buy a gift.

Let me give you another example. I took my staff to lunch at a local restaurant to celebrate something. We use any excuse to have a staff lunch at a nearby restaurant—a birthday, the hiring of a new staff member, a promotion, a visit by an out-of-town colleague. My executive assistant makes a reservation and I pay the tab. I am so grateful for the high quality of my staff that I am eager to appreciate them and they are happy to have so many wonderful restaurant meals to celebrate whatever is the cause of the day. It's a win-win.

At the end of one of these happy restaurant meals, after I had already paid the tab, the waitress came back to me and advised me that a 15 percent gratuity had already been added to the bill because it was a group. She showed me that I had added my own tip on top of the tip that was already part of the bill. She asked me if I had intended to tip her twice. I was startled by her honesty.

I thanked her, and then I deleted my own tip from the credit card tab and left. On the way back to my office I was taken by two different emotions—the joy of being served by such an honest person and the anger at all the other waitresses over the years who had secretively accepted my inadvertent double tip.

I was embarrassed that my honest waitress got less money because of her honesty. What did I do?

I sent a thank-you note to the manager of the restaurant expressing my sincerest appreciation for the honesty of that one wonderful waitress. I am sure she got lots of positive attention from management for that thank-you card. I also expressed my awkwardness at deleting the inadvertent extra tip when she should have been rewarded for honesty, not "punished." I mailed the card and went on with my life.

The next day, personally delivered to our office was a magnificent fruit basket plus a very large certificate for free meals at that restaurant with a warm note signed by the manager.

I felt wonderful. The manager felt wonderful. My staff felt wonderful because they too knew about the story. I am sure the waitress felt wonderful because she was rewarded in some way by that thoughtful manager. And, just possibly, they have also corrected the system of secretly keeping the inadvertent second tip.

Everybody won. The amount of joy and gratitude in the world increased. I balanced my consumption (depreciation) of the restaurant meal with all this gratitude (appreciation). The value of all this happiness is far greater than the actual meal itself. And that is the real meaning of gratitude. That is how, on that day, I balanced consumption of the meal with gratitude, and balanced depreciation with appreciation.

Choose to Improve Your Financial Situation Each Month

Don't work for money; let your money work for you!

Everyone I say this to immediately agrees with me that it is the right way to go. Then, when I ask them what they are going to do the next morning, they reply "Go to work." It is not enough to *know* that you should invest, it is also necessary to *do* it.

However, this third MAINLY pathway of life is not just investing. *Increase in Wealth* means more than just investing.

It also includes

- Reducing your debts
- Creating a financial plan
- Increasing your sales
- Getting more clients
- Networking
- Advertising
- Getting a credit card
- Getting rid of a credit card
- Paying off the balance on a credit card
- Raising your fees or your prices
- Getting a raise if you are employed
- Buying a piece of real estate
- Buying stocks or mutual funds
- Improving your referral system
- Increasing your savings account

- Mortgaging a property
- Paying down a mortgage
- Decreasing the interest rate on your debt
- Increasing the interest rate on your savings
- Selling something you own
- Making a will

Notice that the example of making a will was included in this list for the Increase in Wealth category, and that it was also given in the section on cleaning messes. This is because some goals, like making a will, may be considered to be the cleaning of a mess (if you have worried about it for a while), or a financial goal, or it may actually be in other goal categories as well. If you have never set a goal, it may be in the New category or in the Learn category. The point here is that some tasks could possibly fit into more than one goal pathway, depending on how you view that goal. The most important point I could make about deciding in which category a goal should fit is that you should simply not fret. Choose one appropriate category, and move on.

There are many ways to impact your financial situation. All these ways fall into four basic categories because, as accountants know, there are only four buckets that money can fall into (assets, income, liabilities, or expenses). So, you can:

1. Increase your assets.
2. Increase your income.
3. Decrease your debts.
4. Decrease your expenses.

If you do not consciously improve your financial situation every month, in some way, then the years slip by. A sailboat with no rudder ends up wherever the wind happens to blow.

Clients in my mentoring program tend to be happier than their friends outside the program because they automatically improve their financial situation in some way every month. Sometimes that improvement is minor. That is okay, because the sum total of consistent minor improvements accumulates to a powerfully enhanced financial status.

There rarely is a white knight or silver bullet or magic potion. Yes, occasionally, wonderful opportunities arise and taking advantage of them makes a huge positive difference in your financial situation.

You may win a lottery or inherit a lot of money or buy a penny stock on a hot tip and have it actually skyrocket in price. But those things rarely happen.

You can powerfully bolster your financial situation by making regular, consistent improvements, even of a minor nature, each month. And this approach is guaranteed, without any magic potions.

Aesop, the author of 650 famous fables, taught great moral lessons 2,600 years ago. The wisdom of this lowly slave lives on because of the timeless value of what he wrote. Likely his most famous fable was "The Tortoise and the Hare," wherein he proved that "slow and steady wins the race." It is still true today. Make a financial step, even a small one, *every month*, and you will win.

Choose to Do Something New Each Month

"The only thing constant is change."

This is as true today as when Heraclitus first said it 2,500 years ago. The only difference now is that the rate of change is far more rapid than ever before.

If you are standing still, you are actually slipping backwards.

Life today is a stream flowing slowly against you. To stay in the same place, you must occasionally step forward. To get ahead, stay ahead, and thrive, you must move forward consistently, regularly, and consciously—every month.

How do you do this? The answer is the fourth MAINLY pathway of life: choosing to do something *New* every month. Your world will collapse in on you if you do not consciously expand your horizons.

The rate of discovery and the rate of releasing new products is so rapid these days, that if you stay within your "box," your box will just get relatively smaller and smaller. There will be fewer and fewer options within your shrinking box. There will be fewer ideas for success. There will be less and less flexibility. Ways to overcome obstacles will become continually more restricted. It is your duty to yourself and to your family to continually expand your horizons by doing something new every month.

In The Monthly Mentor™ program, members think of something new every month that they want to have or do that they have not had nor done before. It is a *new way of doing something* or a *new experience.*

Let me give you some examples. In your business life, it could be to:

- Develop a new product or service.
- Improve an existing product or service.
- Get a new computer software program to allow you to do something new.
- Create a web site.
- Offer something new to a client.
- Advertise in a new way.
- Offer a contest or some special new inducement to your clients, and so on.

In your personal life, it could be to:

- Try a different type of restaurant.
- Meet new people.
- Read a new book.
- Read a magazine that you would not normally buy.
- Update your wardrobe.
- Try a new hair style.
- Have some new experience.
- Join a club.
- Begin participating in a new sport.
- Go somewhere new, and so on.

Sometimes the new thing you do may *seem* to make little or no difference in your life. However, each new thing you do opens you up and keeps you open. That alone means success in this fast-changing world. You are now always open to the new opportunities that are emerging all around you.

Also, because you do this every month, you can be assured that some of your new experiences will hit the bull's eye. Relentlessly pursuing a path of investigating something new each month will open your horizons, broaden your scope of options, allow different people to enter your life, eliminate fixed thinking, and in many other ways open you up to the exciting diversity of our planet.

It needs effort and conscious determination to continue this process month after month. One reason that Monthly Mentor™ members are so grateful for the program is that they do not need to wonder whether they have the willpower to keep up this determined effort at experiencing newness each month. It just happens naturally for them because each month they are guided to record a goal in the

New category as one of their six MAINLY goals that month. In this way they stride forward, advancing month after month, effortlessly and consistently. You can do something new right now by going to www .aaron.com/DoubleYourIncome to learn how I can guide you to your own successes.

Choose to Learn Something Each Month

The amount of knowledge is exploding exponentially. And the rate at which it is exploding is also increasing.

Let us go back to about 30,000 B.C. when humans first stood upright. At that time, humans knew just about nothing.

Let us add up everything that was known by every person on Earth at the time of Christ and let us quantify this total amount of knowledge in the world as 1 unit.

We could thus say that the total amount of knowledge in the world when humans first stood upright was 0 and at the time of Christ was 1 unit of worldwide knowledge.

How long did it take for the total amount of knowledge in the world to double to 2 units? It took a millennium and a half, till the year 1500, approximately the era of the Renaissance. To double again to 4 units took the next quarter-millennium, till 1750. To double again to 8 units took only one century, to 1850, around the beginning of the Industrial Revolution. To double again to 16 units took another century, till 1950, just after the Second World War.

Suddenly, in a mere 23 years, because of the invention of the microchip, the total amount of worldwide knowledge did not just double, but rather it doubled and doubled and doubled again—an eightfold increase from 16 units to 128 units—in the brief period from 1950 to 1973.

What is the total amount of knowledge in the world today? The best estimate is a staggering 256,000 units—right off any scale you could have imagined. And even if that number were accurate, it would be too small tomorrow because knowledge is increasing every day. (See Figure 6.1.)

You could never keep up with this mind-boggling explosion of knowledge in every field of discipline. But, you can definitely increase your knowledge every month in *some* way. The fifth MAINLY goal pathway is to *Learn*.

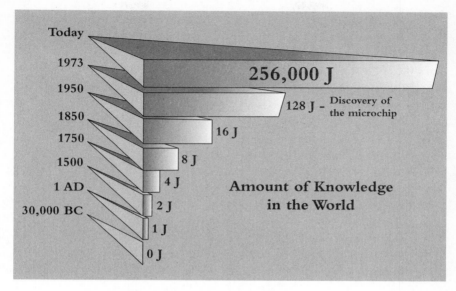

Figure 6.1   Explosive Increase in Knowledge

Examples of what you could learn in your business life might include:

- Becoming more skilled in a certain area
- Taking a course
- Learning a new computer program
- Learning how to operate a new piece of high tech equipment, and so on

In your personal life, examples might include

- Learning a new personal skill
- Reading a nonfiction book
- Watching the Biography Channel or the History Channel
- Taking a personal-growth course
- Learning about a hobby
- Improving yourself in a sport
- Learning how to use your camera or computer better, and so on

We all know that medical doctors these days are bemoaning that their incomes have fallen. We can understand this by understanding the Learn pathway of life.

First, let us look at the amount of knowledge that doctors have. It has fallen over the past several decades in relative terms because there are so many medical discoveries every day in every area of the body and in every illness that a doctor cannot possibly stay up to date with all these advances. So, relative to the total medical knowledge, an individual doctor knows less and less.

Now let's look at patients. Decades ago, patients knew practically nothing about medicine. They did what they were told and took the prescription they were written. Today, many patients visit any one of thousands of free medical advice web sites on the Internet. They come to the doctor's office armed with the latest discoveries related to their illness. They come armed with a list of all the side-effects of the drugs commonly prescribed for their illness. They come armed with a prioritized listing of which of the commonly prescribed drugs are most effective and which have been shown to be less effective. So, patients know relatively much more.

Doctors know less, compared to the expanding vastness of the totality of medical knowledge today. Patients know more, certainly in regard to their own illness. Hence, the difference between the doctor's knowledge and the patient's knowledge is squeezed. Doctors' knowledge (compared with their patients' knowledge) has slipped, and this is why doctors' incomes have fallen.

This is happening in all areas of endeavor. It is not unique to the medical profession. Bookkeepers are struggling because their job has been replaced by a simple computer program. Tellers are struggling because their job has been replaced by an ATM machine. Lawyers' incomes have fallen because computer programs are readily available to do what they charge fees for. And the parade goes on. You must prevent this calamity from happening to you, by continuing to learn.

Choose to Do Something Just for Yourself Each Month

Life has purpose. In this book, we call it My Life Mission™. Whatever is your purpose, you should enjoy your life as you are pursuing it. Enjoying the journey of life is the point of the sixth MAINLY pathway of life: *Yourself.*

My mentored clients are sometimes initially puzzled by this pathway. They do not know what it means. They ask me for advice and examples, showing that they have never put much thought into this important area.

Doing something just for you is *taking care of yourself.* It is treating yourself in some way that is important to you. What would you just love to do? What treat would you love to allow yourself to experience or enjoy? This is the sixth pathway.

In your personal health, examples may include

- Eliminating an addiction
- Beginning an exercise program
- Losing weight
- Reducing fats from your diet
- Reducing sugars from your diet

Examples in other areas of your personal life may include

- Attending a special event
- Fulfilling a childhood dream
- Having fun in some way you particularly enjoy
- Having quiet time
- Reading a great book
- Going on a vacation
- Spending time with special people you don't see often enough
- Pursuing a spiritual quest
- Meditating
- Visiting a place you miss and want to see again
- Visiting a place you've never seen and have always wanted to visit
- Playing your favorite sport more often

Looking back over my life, there are some outstanding examples of what I have done just for myself. I made a decision a long time ago to enjoy an exotic one-week vacation every month. In Chapter 1, "Have It Now!," I told you how you can have that joy every month beginning right now, and that is how I personally began, too. Those vacations have allowed me to be refreshed and eager in the three weeks I work each month. Consequently I produce more value for my many clients in those three weeks per month than I could possibly produce in all four weeks per month of working. My clients have greatly benefited and so have I.

Another thing I did just for myself was to pursue my childhood fantasy of riding a unicycle. I had always dreamed of being able to do it, but I had always just ignored it as a childish dream. When I began to realize that life was about noticing what is truly important to me and enjoying it—regardless of whether it seemed silly to others or even to me—I began the process of learning to ride a unicycle.

It took a year. I worked at it almost every evening and almost every weekend. In the winter months, I used a nearby auditorium where the janitor would let me in to practice. I tried. I fell. I tried. I fell. I took lessons. I tried. I fell.

Then, one grand day, I got up and stayed up. I was a unicyclist! My heart leaped with glee. I count this as one of my happiest accomplishments. It certainly is not as important as helping many of my mentored clients dramatically improve their wealth and other aspects of their lives. It is not as important as being a good father or a good husband or a good boss or a good teacher. But, in my life, it is a blessing. I smile with overflowing joy even just *thinking* of myself riding that unicycle. For years, I actually kept my unicycle in my bedroom so that I could see it all the time.

Was that silly? Absolutely not—I think *silly* is *not* doing what you love and then finding out that it is no longer possible because of an accident, aging, an illness, or some other calamity. I view these pursuits as the spice of life.

What "unicycles" do you have unfulfilled in your life that you need to ride? Think about it and let no one deter you from your path of identifying what you would like to do just for yourself.

You can go to www.aaron.com/DoubleYourIncome to see me riding both a normal unicycle and my favorite 5-foot-tall giraffe unicycle. Yes, I learned how to ride both and I am really proud of it. You'll enjoy this. Do it just for yourself.

FAQs

1. **Why are there six pathways?**
   After decades of mentoring clients to startling successes in their lives, far beyond what they could have ever believed, it has become clear to me that using these six pathways works.

2. **Are these six specific pathways tried and tested?**

   These six pathways have enabled me and thousands of clients to achieve great success. From the practical point of view, these six are certainly worth following. They have stayed constant for many years and have thus withstood the infallible test of time.

3. **Is it okay to set six mess goals and none of the others one month?**

   No. It is important to stride forward in *all six pathways* each month. It is important to maintain balance. It is important to view your life as a whole. Set one goal in each of the six pathways.

4. **Is it okay to set a second mess goal after I have set one goal in each of the six goal pathways?**

   Once you have fulfilled the rule of setting a goal in each of the six pathways of life, you may indeed set another goal in any goal category.

5. **What should I do if I cannot tell which goal fits into which goal pathway?**

   This will often happen. For example, you might want to clean your desktop. It may seem to be a *mess* goal. But, it also could be something wonderful just for *yourself.* You also may feel that it is holding you back from making clear decisions in your business and hence may consider it to be an *increase in wealth* goal. Do you place the goal of cleaning your desk into the M or Y or I pathway? Don't fret; just place it into the most appropriate pathway for you.

6. **What's the difference between the *Learn* and *New* goals?**

   The *learn* goal requires you to *study* something so that you will know something that you did not know before. The *new* goal requires you to *do* something you do not usually do, but it does not necessarily require you to learn anything. For example, one mentored client of mine took a lunch break for the first time ever one month. It was new, but there was nothing to learn.

   I remember once going to a multiscreen theater and listing the movies available in order of my preference. I then consciously chose to see the *last* movie on my list, just to do something new. It was the Arnold Schwarzenegger movie, *Terminator 2.* I knew that it would be a childish "shoot -'em-up movie" filled with absurd and glitzy special effects. I am so glad I chose that movie. It was dazzling and fun. It was not those negatives that I had, with great elitism, prejudged. I had broadened my horizons. My box had been expanded. My self-assuredness had been knocked down a peg or two. And those are the usual benefits of doing something new.

Three Expert Action Steps

You know the dangers of becoming narrow and one-dimensional in life. You know that the solution is following the six MAINLY pathways of life. You know what each pathway is and you have lots of examples of what you might do each month within each pathway.

It is time to use what you have learned. Below are listed the Three Expert Action Steps™ designed to support you in bringing what you have just read into play in your life. Once you have completed these Three Expert Action Steps, you will be ready to move on to the next chapter to learn a novel way to record goals so that you will be *guaranteed* to achieve them.

> **First Expert Action Step: Record any 10 goals and identify in which goal pathway they belong.**
> Find 10 goals you have written, or look at 10 goals used as examples in other chapters in this book. Place each of them into one of the six goal pathways, just for practice in becoming familiar with the MAINLY goal pathways. By way of example, you might say:
> - Cleaning my desktop: M (mess category)
> - Planning a vacation: Y (doing something just for myself)

> **Second Expert Action Step: Select one goal for this month in each of the six goal pathways.**
> For this step, do not write out the whole goal; just record the name of the goal as shown above. It is sufficient to record "Call my mother," "Make my will," and so forth. These are the *titles* of the goals. Select one for each of the six pathways and be sure to select the ones you actually wish to achieve this coming month. You will learn how to record them powerfully in the next chapter.

Third Expert Action Step: Select at least three more goals in each of the six goal pathways.

These additional goals are not intended to be done this coming month but comprise a "warehouse" of goal ideas for future months. For each goal pathway, record the names of several goals you wish to achieve in the near future. Keep this inventory for future reference.

To create a categorized inventory of future goals you wish to eventually achieve, do the exciting exercise available at www.aaron.com/DoubleYourIncome.

Moving On

You know the six MAINLY pathways of life. Chapter 7 will teach you how to write goals in each pathway so that you are guaranteed to achieve them!

CHAPTER 7

Achieve Your Goals for Sure

HOW YOU CAN ACHIEVE EVEN YOUR TOUGHEST GOALS NO MATTER WHAT—GUARANTEED!

Achieve every goal in your life—no matter what!

What a brilliant skill. You would easily become exactly the person you've always wanted to become and have everything you've always wanted to have, if only you had this skill. Yes, if only you had this startling, almost superhuman skill, *wow* what a life you'd have.

You are about to learn the biggest discovery ever made in the arena of goal achievement.

In this chapter you will learn how to achieve any goal you record—*guaranteed!* Even more startling, you will learn how to achieve even your very toughest goals—in some cases without doing any work at all.

Should You Set Large Goals or Small Goals?

Large goals, if achieved, bring enormous results with a burst of pride and self-esteem. But, the biggest goals are rarely achieved. Small goals may be easy to achieve, but so what? Attaining a small goal may not be too significant. So, do we set large goals or small goals?

Now is the time for you to learn the answer to this critically important question so that you can have enormous successes without the fear of failure.

To explain how it works, let me take you back to the summer of 1976 in Montreal, Canada, during the Olympics. I loved attending the Olympics and was particularly intrigued with men's volleyball.

What an exciting game. But, it was not the game that gave me the huge insight. It was not any player or any skillful play that allowed me to come up with an idea that has helped thousands of my clients dramatically improve their ability to record and achieve goals.

Here is what happened. In the finals, the teams that ranked fourth and third played off for the Bronze medal. The team that won was jubilant and the team that lost was understandably disappointed.

Also, in those same finals, the teams that ranked first and second played off for the Gold and Silver medals. The team that won was jubilant and the team that lost was understandably disappointed.

There was nothing unusual about those reactions. My gigantic insight occurred during the awards ceremony. The Gold medal team danced in excitement on the podium. The Silver medal team was dejected and silent. The Bronze medal team was jubilant, giving high-fives to the Gold medal team and waving into the camera to celebrate their success with the world.

This did not make sense to me. Certainly it is better to stand second in the world than third. Yet the second-place team was dejected and the third-place team was ecstatic. Though it did not make sense, there had to be an explanation.

"It is better to win by winning than to win by losing."

—Raymond Aaron

Here is what I deduced. The Gold and Bronze medal winners ended the tournament with a win and were therefore positive. The Silver medal winner ended the tournament with a loss and were therefore negative. The team that won Silver did not, in their mind, actually win Silver; rather, they *lost Gold*.

It is better to win by winning than it is to win by losing. The Gold medal team won their medal by winning. The Bronze medal team won their medal by winning. Unfortunately, the second-place team won their Silver medal by losing. So, it seems that it is better psychologically to win by winning—even if you win third place versus second place.

However, the voice of reason must be inserted here. Certainly, one would think, it is better to win Silver than Bronze, no matter how you feel at the moment. That was my conundrum. Let me restate the problem as a goal problem.

Should you set a very high goal? There is a great advantage to setting a high goal: It will inspire you to reach for the stars. Though you may not reach such lofty heights, you will likely have attained more just because you aimed higher. Yes, that is wonderful. However, like the Silver medal winners, you may not enjoy your success because you win by losing.

Should you set only easy goals? If you do, you will likely achieve them and feel wonderful. But your achievements will be minor. Should you achieve little but feel good, or achieve a lot but feel bad? It's a tough call.

A New Way to Record Goals

As I was trying to find the nugget of truth in this puzzle, another, apparently unrelated, incident happened in my life. I was chatting with a dear colleague, Alan Jacques. We love startling each other with our most prized pieces of wisdom.

He told me about a way to record goals that is different from anything I had ever heard of before. Instead of recording a goal, you subdivide your goal into *three levels of achievement.* The first level is called The Minimum Level™. In this subgoal, you record what you can be *counted on* to do—based not on your hopes, but on your actual history. In other words, this will almost certainly get done. It is not much more than a to-do item. Be sure, though, that it *is* more than a to-do item, so that it really is a goal.

Example of a Goal Written the "Old" Way:

I commit to cleaning my garage by August 15.

Example of the Same Goal Written the "New" Way

I commit to cleaning my garage by August 15 by breaking it into the following three levels:

Minimum: Discard the three old tires.

Target: Discard all broken tools.

Outrageous: Take everything out of the garage, paint the entire garage, and replace only what I really need.

If you can be counted on to achieve it, then it seems like it is just a to-do item, and not really a goal. Just because you can be counted on to achieve it, does not mean that you will definitely achieve it this month. So, it is a goal, even though you can typically be counted on to do it.

The next level is called The Target Level™. This is the stretch beyond what you are confident you can do.

The highest level is called The Outrageous Level™. This is the goal you think you could not possibly achieve. This is wild—this is really *out there*.

The New Raymond Aaron Dictionary of Goal Achievement Terms

Minimum Level: This is the first and easiest of the three goal levels. This is the one you can be counted on to achieve, based on your past history.

Target Level: This is a stretch.

Outrageous Level: This is the most challenging of the three goal levels. This is the one that seems practically impossible to achieve.

An alternative way of defining these three levels is that you have the tools, time, and other resources necessary to achieve The Minimum Level. You know how to get the tools, time, and other resources for The Target Level. For The Outrageous Level, you do not even know (yet) what tools, time, or resources you'll need and certainly do not know (yet) where or how to get them.

Why is this technique so brilliant? First, it solves the Volleyball Olympics problem. You can set an easy (Minimum Level) goal and achieve it and be happy, even though the achievement is small. This relates to the Bronze medal winners.

You also record an Outrageous Level, which will encourage you to stretch toward it and will cause your mind to begin working on a solution for you, even in the background, without your conscious awareness.

Since you are already happy because of the achievement of The Minimum and possibly also The Target Level, you may as well stretch toward The Outrageous Level. If you achieve it, you will have accomplished far more than if you had not set that huge goal.

Get small goodies and feel good. There is no worry that you will be limited to only small successes because you have also set Target and Outrageous levels of that same goal. So, you may also get large goodies and feel even better. But, if you do not get the larger goodies, it is okay, because you've already had a success and you already feel great.

Second, it solves the problem of recording a goal in the standard way ("I commit to cleaning my garage by September 15"). In this way, you either achieve it and feel good or miss it and feel bad. You either get it or you blow it. Using Minimum, Target, and Outrageous levels, everything is set up either for

> *"The secret of getting ahead is getting started. The secret of getting started is breaking your complex overwhelming tasks into small manageable tasks, and then starting on the first one."*
> —Mark Twain

small success or large success—plus enhanced self-esteem at every stage.

In my experience of over 20 years mentoring thousands of eager goal-setters, I often am asked, "If I know for sure I will not have time to work on the Outrageous Level, should I bother recording it?" This is a good question. The answer is clear: a resounding *yes!* Why? Because you may not actually need to work on it consciously to achieve it. My experience is that many of my mentored clients achieve their Outrageous Levels every month—even ones they did not *consciously* work on at all! The Law of Attraction works for you in unforeseen ways.

The topic of the next section is exactly how to achieve goals without actually *consciously* doing anything!

Achieve Goals *Automagically*

Think of one of your unfulfilled desires, possibly one that has been hanging around for years. How can it suddenly and effortlessly get achieved one brief month after recording it on The Monthly Mentor™ forms? How is all this possible when you may not even have consciously worked on the goal and it just seems to have achieved itself on its own?

I have personally witnessed this happening every single month with my mentored clients. Not only do they achieve their goals, sometimes without even consciously working on them, but they sometimes achieve their Outrageous Levels in that way.

Why does this happen? The answer is that your mind is a goal-striving mechanism. You either inherit goals from TV or your parents or colleagues, without conscious direction, or you purposefully set goals. Either way, your mind sets about to achieve these goals.

Think of the puzzling *placebo effect*. Pharmaceutical firms spend billions of dollars to develop a drug to cure a certain human ailment. Then, in testing this drug, they give half the group the experimental drug and the other half the sugar pill, or placebo. Every participant, though, thinks he or she is receiving the real drug. Startlingly, the minds of the participants go to work to fulfill the goal. It always happens that some participants in the placebo group are cured.

Since this phenomenon occurs at the subconscious level and since it happens on its own and since it seems beyond human understanding, I have coined a new word to represent it: I claim you can achieve goals *automagically!*

The New Raymond Aaron Dictionary of Goal Achievement Terms

Automagically (*adv.*) Of or pertaining to the well-documented and ongoing delightful experience of having goals seemingly achieve themselves without conscious effort on the part of the goal-setter.

I make this claim with the firm confidence of having seen this occur thousands of times over a period of two decades of mentoring my clients to achieve their most outrageous goals.

Another way to understand "automagically" is to realize that it is in total harmony with the Law of Attraction. When you record a goal, and put in the additional thinking required to set three levels of that goal, and complete the other sections of the goal-recording form, you have put so much energy and intention into your goal that the Universe springs into action through the Law of Attraction to fulfill your goal, in some cases, for you.

"The tragedy of life doesn't lie in not reaching your goal. The tragedy lies in having no goals to reach."

—Benjamin Mays

Complete your goals on our special forms, following our techniques and rules, and you, too, will have the delightful experience of having your most difficult goals achieve themselves *automagically!*

Automagically and MTO

Now that we have coined the new word, *automagically*, it is time to coin another term to refer to the process of subdividing a goal into three levels. The acronym for the Minimum, Target, and Outrageous levels is MTO™. In The Monthly Mentor program and in my business life, I use it as a noun. For example: "I like this new business idea, Ken. It looks like it could be quite profitable. What is your MTO for profit in its first year?" What I mean by this is: "What are your predictions as to the Minimum, Target, and Outrageous levels of profit that this new venture might produce?"

The New Raymond Aaron Dictionary of Goal Achievement Terms

MTO (*n.*) The Minimum, Target, and Outrageous levels of a goal.

MTO (*v.*) To subdivide a goal into its Minimum, Target, and Outrageous levels.

Without the concept of MTO, we could not even have a worthwhile discussion. Let me explain. If we were brainstorming on a new business, a legitimate question would be: *How much money do you think we will make this year?* One participant might say $100,000. Another might say $1 million.

On the surface, it looks like there is total disagreement. There seems no way to resolve this wide gap. However, MTO solves the dilemma. Using MTO, we learned that those two participants actually had *exactly* the same prediction. How is that possible? The first participant, as a conservative person, was giving his cautious answer, not wanting to tempt the gods by being too eager. The second participant, an overeager entrepreneur, was stating the best possible result.

To resolve the apparent disagreement, I simply asked them not to give their best guess, but rather to give their MTO. In this case, they gave exactly the same reply, when phrased in the MTO format:

Minimum Level	$100,000
Target Level	$500,000
Outrageous Level	$1 million

My friends, colleagues, and mentored clients all talk like this. For example, I may ask my Director of Seminars, "Wendy, how many of my mentored clients do you think will come out to hear my latest presentation on goal-setting next week?" She will promptly reply, "175, 225, 300." Really what I had asked was simply, "What's your MTO for attendance next week?"

So, MTO is a noun, meaning the three levels of a goal. It is also a verb, meaning to subdivide a goal into its three levels. How would I use that? If I am coaching a new member who has just told me his goal without subdividing it into the three levels, I will reply to him: "Please MTO that goal."

The Magic of MTO Is Available in Three Ways

How can you MTO a goal? There are three different ways to subdivide a goal into its three MTO levels:

1. The Nested Technique™
2. The Graduated Technique™
3. The Deadline Technique™

The Nested Technique to MTO a Goal

Minimum Level: I will do 10 sales this month.

Target Level: I will do 20 sales this month.

Outrageous Level: I will do 30 sales this month.

The most common is The Nested Technique. In this procedure, you state The Minimum Level that you are confident you can achieve based on your actual history. Then The Target Level is The Minimum Level plus even more. The Outrageous Level is The Target Level plus even more. So, if you achieve The Target Level, you've also automatically achieved The Minimum Level. If you achieve The Outrageous Level, you've also automatically achieved The Target and Minimum Levels.

The Graduated Technique to MTO a Goal

Minimum Level: I will help Laura.
Target Level: I will help Michelle.
Outrageous Level: I will help James.

Minimum Level: I will clean the garage.
Target Level: I will plant a garden.
Outrageous Level: I will finish the deck.

A second way to MTO a goal is simply deciding on three different tasks, each one more challenging *for you* than the previous one, that are not necessarily related to each other. Let's say you enjoy working with Michelle and Laura, but it is not always easy to find time in Michelle's busy schedule to meet with her. And, you find James quite a challenge to work with. For whatever reason, it is easiest to help Laura, tougher to help Michelle, and toughest to help James. If you help James but not Michelle or Laura, then you have achieved The Outrageous Level but not your Minimum or Target Levels.

In the second example of The Graduated Technique, our enthusiastic goal-setter believes that finishing the deck is the toughest task he could tackle in his home; planting a garden is a little easier but still a big stretch; but he is sure he can clean the garage, based on his past track record.

The third technique to MTO a goal is the least used, probably because it is the most scary. It is the Deadline Technique, wherein you simply move the deadline closer and closer to create the higher levels of MTO while keeping the content of the goal the same.

The Deadline Technique to MTO a Goal

Minimum Level: I will make my first sale by January 30.

Target Level: I will make my first sale by January 15.

Outrageous Level: I will make my first sale by January 5.

For example, you may be chatting with your spouse about when you want to take your next big vacation. Of course, neither of you knows now exactly when it will be. It depends on your job demands, the kids' schedules, and saving enough money. Nevertheless, you can still MTO the date of your intended vacation. You may record secretly on a piece of paper:

Minimum Level: Christmas of next year

Target Level: Summer of next year

Outrageous Level: Christmas of this year

Your spouse also records MTO dates. You then share your thoughts.

Interestingly, your spouse may have selected practically the same deadlines. This gives you some comfort that you are thinking the same thoughts.

Alternatively, you each may have selected totally different deadline dates. This means that you have different assumptions or aspirations about your different futures. Knowing this can lead to valuable discussions. It may be that the wife cannot envision leaving on a big trip until a certain family function is held, whereas the husband wanted to intentionally have the trip before that family event, for another very valid reason. The MTO thus was able to bring them closer to the real issue.

The New Raymond Aaron Dictionary of Goal Achievement Terms

The Nested Technique: In this way to MTO a goal, The Target Level includes The Minimum Level and The Outrageous Level contains the other two.

The Graduated Technique: In this way to MTO a goal, The Minimum Level is the easiest, The Target Level is tougher, and The Outrageous Level is the toughest—even though these three subgoals may be unrelated to each other.

The Deadline Technique: This way to MTO a goal relates not to the content of the goal but to the completion date. The Minimum Level deadline is furthest away; The Target Level deadline is closer; and The Outrageous Level deadline is closest.

Achieving Goals Guaranteed

Let's review the promise of the subtitle of this chapter: *How you can achieve even your toughest goals no matter what—guaranteed!*

There are four ways that this occurs. First, no matter how gigantic it is, when you MTO your goal, you will likely achieve your Minimum Level and hence have achieved a goal. The way to eat an elephant is one bite at a time.

Second, achieving your Minimum Level is so inspiring that you will likely be moved to work toward your higher levels within the goal, and therefore achieve even more of your goal.

Next, note that goal recording is not a once-only event. Goal recording is a monthly habit, at least among my mentored clients. We find that if we achieve nothing at all one month, but record the same goal for the next month, we may well achieve a considerable amount of that goal in the second month. Our subconscious has been working under the surface during that first "unsuccessful" month, and the fruits of that internal subconscious work emerge as success in the outer world in the subsequent month.

Finally, take the example of achieving your Minimum Level one month. It seems like an insignificant step, but any step toward a goal that has eluded you for a long time is valuable. When you record next month's goals, you may find that your levels have cascaded down. In other words, last month's unattained Target Level is this month's

Minimum Level. Similarly, last month's unattained Outrageous might now be this month's Target.

It is in these four ways that goals seem to achieve themselves in The Monthly Mentor program.

FAQs

1. **How easy should the Minimum Level be?**

   That is a great question and an easy one to answer. It needs to be as easy as required to ensure that you achieve it. The purpose is to have the success. This level is not a stretch. It is the guaranteed success we need to feel good and keep going. If you are consistently missing The Minimum Level of your goal, set it easier and easier until you begin to achieve it consistently.

   This is the hardest instruction for the "Type A" overachievers who come to me for mentoring. They feel demeaned setting an easy Minimum Level. I tell them that no matter how embarrassed they might be by how easy it seems, if that is the most they can be counted on to achieve based on their track record, then that is the most they are permitted to record as their Minimum Level.

2. **How often will I achieve a goal *automagically* without even working at it?**

   When you complete your goals on the special forms available at www.aaron.com/DoubleYourIncome and when you follow the rules for recording goals, you will be surprised at how often your goals get achieved, even without your consciously working at them. You want a number? There are no numbers. But, I can promise you that it will be higher than you can now imagine and that you will be surprised that it even happens at all.

3. **Do I have to record all three levels for every goal, even if only two seem more appropriate?**

   Yes. Let me give you an example. Emma wanted to pass an exam to become qualified as a health practitioner. Her Minimum Level was passing. Her Target Level was getting first-class honors. She wondered what else there could be. After I told her that she had to record an Outrageous Level, she hesitantly suggested "standing first in the class," but she was not motivated to stand first in the class nor would it have brought her any advantage. So, that idea really did not work. She was stuck. I insisted that she keep thinking.

She finally came up with "getting offered a job in the field." It was so Outrageous that she laughed but she admitted that that was what she really wanted. I acknowledged her for her creativity. Emma e-mailed me one month later. She passed. She did not achieve first-class honors. But, she got a job! She got her M and her O, but not her T.

4. **In the Graduated Technique, is it possible to achieve The Outrageous Level but not The Target or Minimum Levels?**
Yes. It often happens. This has puzzled me for years. My mentored clients were sometimes achieving the higher

"It's easier to hit an elephant than an ant."

—Raymond Aaron

levels and missing the lower levels. That did not at first make sense to me. Here is my best explanation.

The Outrageous Level has more "juice," more excitement. It is easier to focus on a big goal. It is easier to dream about a big goal. It is easier to tell our friends about a big goal. So it sometimes happens (to our shock) that the big goal gets achieved and the ones we had deemed easier do not. Interestingly, this is in total alignment with The Law of Attraction: The more focused energy and intention you put into something, even inside your mind, the greater is the instruction to the Universe to manifest it for you.

5. **How far away should my goal deadlines be?**
Life progresses in months. The moon cycles in months. Months are so important that they are named, whereas years are just numbered and weeks are neither named nor numbered. This seems to indicate that the ancients realized the heightened significance of monthly cycles. We must respect this age-old wisdom. In The Monthly Mentor, we set goals every month.

Nevertheless, if what you want will legitimately require more than a month to complete, simply write a goal to accomplish an important *part* of it within the month. For example, if you wish to double your profits this year, then ask yourself what you could do *this month* toward that annual goal. For example, you may choose to launch a sales contest this month or you may aim to make 10 new sales this month. These monthly goals are the appropriate goals to record in service of your annual desire.

Also, in The Monthly Mentor, we set *strategic* goals each year, not just monthly goals. This concept will be covered in depth in the chapter entitled, "Annual Backwards Goals." Why are they "backwards"? You will learn the fascinating answer in Chapter 10.

Three Expert Action Steps

You know the great value of recording goals in the MTO format. You know how to record a goal that you will achieve for sure. You know how to record an outrageous goal, one that is lofty and worth aiming at but that won't leave you crushed if you fail to achieve it. You know three different ways to MTO goals. You have learned about the word *automagically*, which describes the experience you are about to have when goals you record using these principles actually get achieved, sometimes effortlessly. You have learned a new way to talk about the future, by phrasing your predictions in the MTO format. You know how to invoke the powerful Law of Attraction by recording your goals on the special Monthly Mentor form available at www.aaron .com/DoubleYourIncome.

It is time to use what you have learned. Below are listed the Three Expert Action Steps™ designed to support you in bringing what you have just learned into play in your life. Once you have completed these Three Expert Action Steps, you will be ready to move on to Chapter 8, where you will learn to record your goals correctly.

> **First Expert Action Step: Record a goal in the MTO format using the Nested Technique.**
> Select a goal. Nest the MTO levels so that the Target Level is bigger than the Minimum Level and the Outrageous Level is bigger than the Target Level.

> **Second Expert Action Step: Record a different goal in the MTO format using the Graduated Technique.**
> Here are the stages in recording a goal using the Graduated Technique:
>
> 1. Select a goal. Let's say it is cleaning your office.
> 2. Next select a deadline, say August 15, within a one-month timeframe, certainly no longer.

3. Decide on The Minimum, Target, and Outrageous levels that represent graduated tasks. Let's say you decide to clean everything off your desktop as the minimum. This is easy, as you do it often. Then you want to clean out the unneeded papers from the top drawer of your filing cabinet. This has always bothered you and you seem to never get around to doing it. Finally, it would be a miracle if you could buy a modern filing cabinet with color-coded hanging files inside.

For example:

I commit to achieving a goal related to *cleaning my office* by *August 15* by breaking it into the following three levels:
Minimum Level: I will *clean my desktop.*
Target Level: I will *discard old papers from the top drawer.*
Outrageous Level: I will *buy a filing cabinet with color-coded files.*

Third Expert Action Step: Record yet another goal in the MTO format using the Deadline Technique.
Select a goal on a different topic. Select a goal you are confident you can achieve by a certain date, as this will become your Minimum Level, and then think of dates before that for The Target and Outrageous levels.

Moving On

You are ready to move to the next chapter, in which you will learn to record your goals correctly, according to The Six Goal-Recording Rules™. When you correctly record your goals, you most powerfully invoke the wonderful Law of Attraction.

CHAPTER 8

The Six Goal-Recording Rules

HOW YOU CAN RECORD GOALS THE RIGHT WAY SO THEY EFFORTLESSLY INVOKE THE LAW OF ATTRACTION

"You are both seventy years old and you have been married for fifty years. Congratulations. As the Good Fairy, I am here to grant each of you one wish."

The wife immediately replied: "We have always wanted to go on a glorious vacation. So, I would like to share my one wish with my lifelong partner and take him on a wonderful first-class, two-month cruise around the world in perfect health." As soon as she completed her sentence, travel tickets magically appeared on the table in front of them—exactly what she had wished for.

Then the Good Fairy looked at the husband. He sheepishly replied: "I am really sorry to have to say this. I know she has been a wonderful wife for half a century and I know she shared her only wish with me, but really, what I want is a wife thirty years younger than me."

As soon as he finished his sentence, he instantly became 100 years old.

The moral is that if you record your goals inaccurately, you will not get what you want—even if you are guaranteed success. Using the techniques explained in this book, you are indeed guaranteed success. But what success will you get? You will get what you literally ask for, which may not be what you intended or wanted.

There is yet another downside. You may write your goals in such a way that no one can even tell if you've achieved them. This sounds absurd, but it is actually the most common error in recording goals, as you will soon learn.

It is critically important to record goals correctly. What are the rules for correct recording? When I searched the literature, I found nothing. So, I embarked on groundbreaking research to uncover, for the first time ever, the rules for correctly recording goals. There are huge lessons in this research for you. When you obey the rules for proper recording, you will find that your goals begin to achieve themselves *automagically!*

Discovering How to Record Goals the Right Way

When I investigated the rules for correctly recording goals, I asked my 300 closest clients to record 10 goals each. I gave them no conditions or rules. I just asked them to record and submit to me 10 goals each. When all 3,000 goals were received, I assembled a *Goal-Recording Research Team* of eager but totally unprepared colleagues. Why were they unprepared? Because no one had ever attempted to uncover these rules, so neither they nor I knew what to do.

There were six of us on this team. We photocopied the 3,000 goals so that each member of the team had a copy of the whole set of goals. My vague instruction to the team was: "Read all goals and circle in red any goal that does not seem to be correct and print beside that goal what seems to be wrong." Since I did not know any more, I could not be any clearer at the time.

We met again when we had done our work. I was startled. Though we had no formal framework, we did nevertheless have a good sense of what was right and what was not. How do I know this? Because, one by one, we went through the whole set of 3,000 goals. When a goal was good, all six of us would agree. If one of us thought that a goal was bad, the most common experience was that all six thought the goal was bad. Sometimes we had a good idea of what was wrong; often we had only a vague notion.

As we journeyed through the 3,000 goals, we began to notice interesting patterns. We began to see similar problems recurring. We began to place problematic goals into "buckets" where all of them exhibited the same "error"—even if we could not yet exactly name the error. As we reviewed all the goals in each bucket, we were able to identify the actual error that we had sensed but could not necessarily name at the beginning of the journey.

After many hours of arduous but exhilarating meetings, we completed studying all 3,000 goals and placing all badly written goals into buckets. There were six buckets. In other words, *there were six ways to write a goal badly.*

We then wrote one rule for each type of error, so that we had the *Six Goal-Recording Rules*™—*never before compiled.*

Some goals were written so badly that they actually exhibited as many as four goal-recording errors in one brief sentence. We were impressed at how so many errors could be squeezed into so few words!

That was Phase I of the process. Phase II involved bringing together again all 300 participants and teaching them the Six Goal-Recording Rules. They loved what they learned. They practiced each rule and I answered questions until every participant understood the rules perfectly. Then, I gave the next assignment: Record and submit another 10 goals each. This time the team was easily able to race through the new 3,000 goals, quickly identifying the incorrectly recorded goals.

We learned some fascinating lessons:

- There were significantly fewer incorrect goals in the second batch—meaning that learning these rules definitely helps.
- Though there were fewer errors, there still were errors—meaning that you must constantly be on your guard to be accurate when you record goals.
- There were *no new error types* in the second batch—meaning that we had found every possible goal-recording rule.

This was an exciting journey of discovery and success—it yielded a valuable tool that would bring a great benefit to eager goal-setters around the world.

My mentored clients were particularly grateful for these rules. They received the list in printed form. There are two ways you can get these Six Goal-Recording Rules:

1. They are all explained in detail in this chapter.
2. You may download a free printer-friendly copy from www. aaron.com/DoubleYourIncome.

Study these rules. But remember the lesson of Phase II of the research: If you are not *continually* vigilant, you may slip back and begin recording goals poorly again. When you have finished this chapter, make a commitment to yourself to reread it to ensure you really have captured the ideas. You may also wish to keep a copy of the rules in the place where you record your goals.

Here are the Six Goal-Recording Rules:

1. The Deadline Rule

You know you need a deadline, but you also must ensure that it is a good deadline. As simple and as obvious as the Deadline Rule™ is, it is the most violated:

> **No:** *I will finish reading my book.*
> **Yes:** *I will finish reading my book by June 11.*

You know that goals should have deadlines, but I say that goals have to have the *right* deadline.

We noticed that the most common deadlines used by our participants were:

- Month-end
- Year-end
- Their own birthday

What is inappropriate about these dates? Think about it. Do you really want to paint the back porch in the depths of winter on December 31? Do you really want to be installing a toilet in the basement suite on your birthday?

Another deadline error is using vague deadlines. For example, if you say you will do a certain thing by *month-end*, it isn't clear exactly what month you're talking about. If you look at that goal several months later, you don't know exactly when you were supposed to have done it.

Now, think about how clear the following is, because it's done correctly:

> **Example:** *I will clean my garage by July 15.*

This is very clear, and eliminates all vagueness and inappropriateness.

2. Measurable

To know whether you have achieved your goal, it must be *measurable*.

You've probably heard that goals have to be measurable, but I am stricter than you have ever imagined.

You may write goals like, *I will be nicer,* or *I'll be nicer to my spouse.* Who's to say you are nicer? Maybe some days you are nicer and some days you are not. Maybe you did three things that were nicer and one thing that was not. If I asked your spouse just after you did the one thing that was not nicer, maybe your spouse would say you were not nicer. It is just too vague and open to interpretation. So if your goal is to be nicer, but niceness is a little tough to measure, what I would like you to do is concentrate on a specific task that you *could* do.

For example, write a poem. It doesn't even have to be a long poem. You could buy a card and write a little poem in it yourself. For example, *I will write a love poem to my spouse by July 15* is very clear and not open to any interpretation whatsoever. If I called you at midnight on July 15 and said, "Were you nicer to your spouse?," maybe you would say "yes"; maybe you would say "no"; maybe you would say "sometimes." If I asked your spouse the same question, who knows what the answer would be? But if I asked at midnight on July 15, "Did you write a love poem to your spouse?," the answer is either *yes* or *no.* There is no room for interpretation or guesswork.

Every time you are thinking of writing a goal that is in the emotional arena, think of a specific, measurable task you could do that would go toward the emotion that you are trying to create.

Another goal people tend to incorrectly write is *I will be rich,* or *I won't be in as much debt,* or vague statements like that. My suggestion is you write something like this: *I will have $10,000 in my savings account by July 15.*

There are also certain words that are inherently vague. For example, *I will buy a home by a certain date.* The reason this is not measurable is because the word *buy* is open to interpretation. Does "buy" mean that you have submitted an offer? Does "buy" mean you have submitted an offer, and the Realtor says it will probably be accepted? Does it mean that the offer has been accepted, but it hasn't closed yet? Or does "buy" mean that it is closed but you haven't got the keys yet? Or does it mean it is closed and you have the keys, but you haven't moved in yet? Or does it mean you have actually bought it and moved in? You see that all of these outcomes, right from submitting an offer to moving in, could be two or three months separated in time. The verb *buy* has several months' worth of vagueness in it, so it is not measurable.

You might imagine that I'm being too picky. But any time you record a vague goal, you rob yourself of the self-esteem you earn by writing a goal in a completely clear way so that you know whether you got it.

It is better to be clear that you didn't get a goal rather than to be vague about whether you got it. Put lots of attention into writing a goal accurately so that at the end of the time period you can stand up and say, "I got it!" or "I didn't get it."

Another issue is that the goal has to be measurable *on* the deadline. What does that mean? Here's an actual goal that one of my clients recorded: *I will start a business by July 15 that makes $100,000 a year profit.* The problem is that if I call her at midnight on July 15 and say, "Have you started a business that makes $100,000 a year?" the only possible answer she can give me is, "Yes, I started it, but how does anyone know how much money it's going to make? Call me in a year and I'll tell you." That vagueness robs you of the increased self-esteem that you could have had by simply writing the goal correctly.

You need to write the goal in such a way that on July 15, you can tell whether you've achieved it. Here's an example: *I will have received payments from two clients in my new business by July 15.* I can call you on July 15 and say, "Do you have two paying clients in your business?" The answer is either *yes* or *no*. It is measurable on the deadline.

3. Brief

Goals must be brief. Exclude stories.

Do not use *and,* because that just clumps two different goals into one jumbo goal. If you achieve one half and not the other half, then you cannot tell whether you have accomplished the goal. Write it, rather, as *two* goals.

What I have noticed in reviewing goals submitted to me by my clients is that the briefer the goal, the greater the chance that it is a well-written goal. In other words, anything that is a story needs to be eliminated from the goal. Also, the word *and* creates two goals masquerading as one goal.

In order to achieve brevity, eliminate the *story*. Here's an example of a goal that has a story in it: *I will call my mother by August 15 because I feel guilty*, or even worse, *I will finally call my mother.* The word *finally* is a story and *because I feel guilty* is a story. The goal should be written as succinctly as possible: *I will call my mother by August 15.* That's it.

Also avoid the dreaded *and*, because that's a huge brevity stealer: *I will train hard and run a 10K by May 2.* The problem with that goal is that maybe you'll train really hard, but you won't run a 10K by May 2. So if I call you at midnight on May 2 and say, "Did you train hard and run a 10K by May 2?," you are unsure.

Make your goals as succinct as possible, which means no story and get rid of those dreaded *and*s. The goal should simply be: *I will run a 10K by May 2.* You might reply to me that you want to train hard. If that is the case, then write a separate goal on that topic, like *I will join a running club by April 1*, or *I will jog at least three miles four times this month.*

4. The Goal Must Be the Intended Result

Poorly written goals are the *formula to calculate* the result or the *effort required* to get the result. Go for the *result.*

When I teach this, members usually give me a quizzical look. They say, "Well, of course, the goal is the intended result; that's what a goal is—the intended result." Though it seems obvious, this is one of the most common errors.

For example, one of the most common goals is, *I will get a 10 percent raise.* Well, a 10 percent raise isn't the intended result; a 10 percent raise is the formula for *calculating* the intended result. The problem is that the mind can't focus on 10 percent. There's nowhere you can go in your imagination to *see* 10 percent. It's too vague a concept. It's a calculation requirement.

What is the better way? *I will get a raise to $55,000 a year by June 30.* Now, you can focus on $55,000. You can focus on a letter from your employer saying, "Mr. Smith has worked for our firm for six years and is currently earning $55,000 annual salary." That's clear.

Instead of correctly recording, *I will weigh, at most, 180 pounds*, you might incorrectly record the effort required to get there. For example, you may record *I will go on a diet.* The diet isn't the goal. The diet is not the intended result. The diet is the effort required for, or the route to, the intended result.

You may record, *I will buy a car by a certain date.* People inherit cars, people win cars in the lottery, people get given a car by a relative or a friend; all kinds of strange things can happen. I know it won't happen that often, but why prevent it by your word choice? That's the Law of Attraction. Why not write your goals in such a way that you allow the Universe to give you blessings that may only come a few times per lifetime. Even if they come only a few times per lifetime, let them in.

Instead of writing, *I will buy a car,* it's better to write, *I will have a car.* Because *buy a car* is the effort required to do it or the route to get there. But it's not the buying of the car that you want; it's the *owning* of the car. It is not the *going on the diet;* it's the *weighing at most the certain weight* that you want.

Look very carefully at the verbs you use so you are sure you're recording the intended result, and not the work you have to do to get there or the effort or the calculation to get there.

This is not good: *In my stock-trading account I want to earn 5 percent per month profit.* That's not a well-written goal, because sometimes you'll make 7 percent, sometimes you'll lose 2 percent, and you won't even know whether you've attained your goal by the end of the year. If you have \$100,000 in a stock-trading account right now, it's better to record the goal, *By the end of the year, I will have \$160,000 in my stock-trading account,* as opposed to, *I will get a 5 percent profit each month.*

5. Positive

The human mind cannot contemplate the absence of something, so it is self-defeating to write goals about losing weight, stopping smoking, reducing debt. The goal must be stated *positively* so that you can focus on what you want, not what you don't want.

For example, if I say to you, "Do not think about a pink elephant. Whatever you do, do *not* think of a pink elephant. And if by chance you happen to think of a pink elephant, please do not think of a pink elephant with purple polka dots—not purple polka dots." So, of course, all you can do is think of pink elephants with purple polka dots. Why did you do that? *I just told you not to!* There are many things you could have thought about—you could have thought about automobiles or birds or giraffes or black cats or computers. You could have thought about anything else, but the only thing you did think about is the thing I told you not to. When you tell somebody not to think about something, you're drawing attention to it, and the only thing they can do, therefore, is to *think* about it.

For example, if you say that your goal is to stop smoking, the only thing you're going to be thinking about is, you guessed it, smoking. If you want to *stop smoking*, it's far wiser to say, *I will breathe clean air,* or *By February 15, I will have breathed only clean air for one entire week.* Now you're focusing on a lot more than just the cessation of smoking; now you're thinking of going to parks, or making sure you take a walk each day in fresh air. It's a far brighter and wiser perspective than to be just concentrating on trying not to smoke.

I will lose 10 pounds. Where do you go to visualize the absence of 10 pounds? There is nowhere to go. You can't look at your stomach and try to find the absence of 10 pounds. Furthermore, it's a difficult goal to measure because if you recorded a goal, *I will lose 10 pounds by a certain date,* and then I call you on that date and say, "Have you lost 10 pounds?" You're likely reply would be, "Well, I don't remember exactly what I weighed when I wrote it down." So, instead of saying, *I will lose 10 pounds,* it is far wiser to record as your goal, *I will weigh, at most, 180 pounds by July 15.*

Another badly written goal is, *I will pay down my credit card by $1,000.* There's nowhere to go to focus on the reduction of $1,000; it's too vague a concept. You might say, "I know what I had on my credit card on a certain day and I'll just subtract $1,000; I know what it means," but that's just the formula for getting there. Record what it is that you desire. For example, look at the clarity of *My credit card debt will be, at most, $14,000 by April 15.* Then there's no issue of trying to focus on the missing $1,000, or trying to remember what your credit card balance was a month ago.

Eliminate all the stories; eliminate focusing on the negative. Write goals in the positive only:

- *I will breathe only clean air for one week by February 15.*
- *I will weigh, at most, 180 pounds by July 15.*
- *My credit card debt will be, at most, $14,000 on April 15.*

Notice how *clear* and *positive* and *measurable* those statements are.

6. The Dreaded Per

Watch how you record goals requiring you to do a repetitive task. Unfortunately, it seems natural to write, *I will exercise five times per week,* or *I will read a book a month,* or *I will follow my diet every single day.* The problem with this unforgiving method of recording goals is that if you fail once, then you cannot recover for the rest of the period.

> **No:** "I will read a book a month."
> *If you do not read a book in the first month, the whole year is lost.*
> **Yes: "I will read 12 books this year."**
> *Now, you can recover from a bookless month.*
> **No:** "I will jog 3 times per week."
> **Yes: "I will jog 12 times this month."**

I suggest you record the total number of times you will do a certain task and then keep track on your calendar.

In summary, the most powerful way to write goals is to follow these Six Goal-Recording Rules:

1. The right deadline
2. Measurable
3. Brief
4. Intended result (not a calculation)
5. Positive
6. The total number (not the dreaded *per*)

These six Goal-Recording Rules will enable you to get what you want by recording your goals correctly.

FAQ

1. **How can I tell whether a goal obeys every one of the Six Goal-Recording Rules?**
   You can keep the list of rules nearby. And you can ask yourself the critically important question: "If Raymond phones me on the deadline date of this goal and asks whether I have achieved the goal *as written*, will I be able to say either *yes* or *no*, or will I be forced to tell a story?"

Three Expert Action Steps

You know the great value of correctly recording your goals. You know the Six Goal-Recording Rules. You have seen several examples of badly written goals and you have seen the corrections to these errors. You have seen goals that violate a rule. You have experienced within yourself how much more focused you are when you read a correctly recorded goal versus reading a poorly written goal. You have realized that recording a goal the right way actually aids you in achieving it and certainly aids you in determining whether you have achieved it.

It is time to use what you have learned. Below are listed the Three Expert Action Steps™ designed to support you in bringing what you have just read into play in your life. Once you have completed these Three Expert Action Steps, you will be ready to move on to the next stage, which is to record your goals on the special forms I have created to support you in both recording your goals correctly and achieving them more easily by activating the Law of Attraction.

First Expert Action Step

Record a real goal in your life that obeys Goal-Recording Rule #1. Record a different goal that obeys Goal-Recording Rule #2. Continue this for each of the Six Goal-Recording Rules.

Second Expert Action Step

Review at least 10 goals you had previously recorded before reading this chapter, identifying the Goal-Recording Rules that they disobey and rewriting them correctly.

Third Expert Action Step

Review the Six Goal-Recording Rules next month when you record your next set of goals.

Moving On

Now you have earned the right to be introduced to the famous MAINLY™ form, used by all Monthly Mentor™ members around the world. This form is the culmination of all the lessons learned so far in this book. It is a fill-in-the-blanks way to record goals correctly so that they begin to achieve themselves *automagically*!

Remember, you can download a printer-friendly version of the Goal-Recording Rules at www.aaron.com/DoubleYourIncome.

CHAPTER 9

Recording Goals So They Achieve Themselves Automagically

HOW YOU CAN EMPLOY THE LAW OF ATTRACTION TO ACHIEVE YOUR OWN GOALS, SEEMINGLY EFFORTLESSLY

"It came true. I got it. It happened!"

This is the cry of joy I hear every month from my mentored clients around the world. When they record their goals, using the rules and forms developed within The Monthly Mentor™ program, their goals often achieve themselves *automagically*. Without even realizing it, they are using the Law of Attraction and the Universe responds by delivering on their request.

The Universe is a mail-order catalog with free delivery!

Sure, you should work on your goals. However, in addition to that, sometimes your dreams will just show up. The frequency of your Outrageous goals achieving themselves will shock you, when you diligently, accurately, and neatly record your goals on the special MAINLY™ form.

The MAINLY form is the culmination of over two decades of my teaching principles that really work. It is the grand finale of bringing together the many ways of allowing the Law of Attraction to support you in achieving your goals.

Just to remind you, the acronym MAINLY represents the six goal pathways of life:

M: cleaning a *mess* every month

A: expressing a heartfelt *acknowledgment* every month

I: *increasing your wealth* every month

N: doing something *new* every month

L: ensuring that you *learn* something every month

Y: doing something just for *yourself* every month

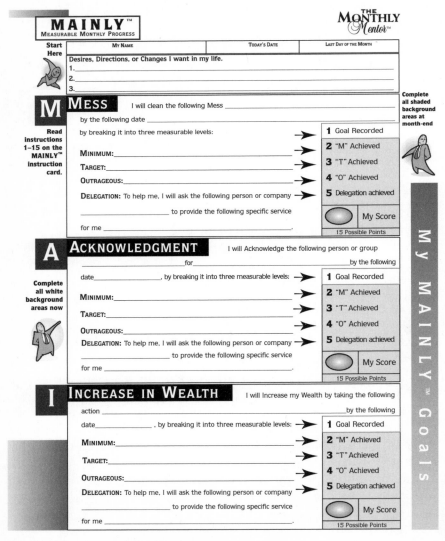

Figure 9.1   Blank MAINLY™ Form

MEASURABLE MONTHLY PROGRESS

N NEW

I will take the following New action _____

by the following date _____

by breaking it into three measurable levels: ➤

MINIMUM:_____ ➤

TARGET:_____ ➤

OUTRAGEOUS:_____ ➤

DELEGATION: To help me, I will ask the following person or company ➤

_____ to provide the following specific service

for me _____.

1	Goal Recorded
2	"M" Achieved
3	"T" Achieved
4	"O" Achieved
5	Delegation achieved

My Score

15 Possible Points

L LEARN

I will Learn about _____

by the following date _____

by breaking it into three measurable levels: ➤

MINIMUM:_____ ➤

TARGET:_____ ➤

OUTRAGEOUS:_____ ➤

DELEGATION: To help me, I will ask the following person or company ➤

_____ to provide the following specific service

for me _____.

1	Goal Recorded
2	"M" Achieved
3	"T" Achieved
4	"O" Achieved
5	Delegation achieved

My Score

15 Possible Points

Y YOURSELF

Just for myself, I will _____

by the following date _____

by breaking it into three measurable levels: ➤

MINIMUM:_____ ➤

TARGET:_____ ➤

OUTRAGEOUS:_____ ➤

DELEGATION: To help me, I will ask the following person or company ➤

_____ to provide the following specific service

for me _____.

1	Goal Recorded
2	"M" Achieved
3	"T" Achieved
4	"O" Achieved
5	Delegation achieved

My Score

15 Possible Points

Enjoy
Measurable
Monthly
Progress!

MY SIGNATURE

....

RATING MY PROGRESS

0-6.......A REST MONTH
7-15.....SOME PROGRESS
16-29...GOOD PROGRESS
30-44...OUTSTANDING PROGRESS
45+.......EXTREME SUCCESS

MY PROGRESS THIS MONTH

Figure 9.1 (Continued)

Obtain a copy of the special MAINLY form for recording goals (see Figure 9.1):

- Photocopy both pages of Figure 9.1 (somewhat smaller than the original because of the page size of this book).
- Download a full-sized, full-color, printer-friendly version from www.aaron.com/DoubleYourIncome.

You now get to combine everything you've learned to record your goals in a very special and powerful way.

Neatly print your name and today's date where shown at the top of the form. In the next space, enter the last day of the month. Now that we have the header information recorded, it is time for you to create an overview for the month.

Three Most Important Results

Every ship needs a rudder. In goal-setting, the rudder is the *three most important results* you wish to create in your life. Note that these desired results are not necessarily results you want to accomplish this month. You may desire to be a wiser person. You may desire to get out of debt, or launch your own business, or get fit, or be married to your soulmate. These are all wonderful desires and totally valid for recording in this section.

The purpose is twofold. First, it alerts the Universe to begin activating the Law of Attraction on your behalf. When you record, with heart and emotion, what you *really desire*, then the Universe listens. Second, it provides a rudder or an overview for the goals you are about to record in the remainder of this special form.

Let me give you an example. If you record a desire to be a wiser person, then you may wish to select a *Y* goal to read a certain nonfiction book this month or join a book discussion club this month. If you record a desire to launch a business, which may not actually occur for some time, you could record a goal to take a business course this month.

Let your mind be free of restrictions. Contemplate where you would truly love to be in your life. What success would you most like to have? What improvement would you most like to put in place?

Relieve yourself of any necessity to record these results in a specific way. You do not need a deadline for the results. The results do not need to be measurable. These are just results you wish to aim for.

For example, results might be:

- I want a better relationship with my spouse.
- I want to laugh a lot.
- I want an improved financial situation.

These are *unacceptable* as goals for all the reasons presented in Chapter 8, "The Six Goal-Recording Rules." But, the three most important results are not goals—they are just a wonderful vision toward which you will aim with your goals.

These desired results are like the horizon. You never get to the horizon, but you can see it and you can aim for it. And, most important, you can record goals that will move you toward the horizon.

Record three such results that you would love to see take place in your life.

The *Umm* Technique versus the Focused Technique for Selecting Goals

We are now at the point of selecting an actual goal to achieve for the upcoming month, in fact, six goals—one in each of the six MAINLY pathways of life.

There are two ways to do it: randomly and strategically. I call the random process the *umm* technique. I call the strategic process the *focused* technique.

The *umm* technique requires you to say *Umm* . . . out loud as you roll your head around in contemplation. After an appropriate period of hemming and hawing, you simply stumble onto a goal you would like to achieve. Though this technique is presented for humor only, it is nevertheless the most common process actually used to select a goal.

That is not your process any longer. You will soon have a *strategic* way of generating the most significant goal for you.

You have five strategic sources from which to draw ideas for goals:

1. Your Annual Love Letters™
2. Your Life Missions™
3. Your three most important results from the top of this MAINLY form
4. Your Annual Backwards Goals™
5. Your Future Generator™

Reviewing your Annual Love Letters will remind you which loves you wish to experience more fully. You may wish to strategically select a goal that supports your enjoying one of these loves.

Reviewing your Life Missions will help you select goals that move you strategically forward toward your life's purpose.

Heeding your desires, you should definitely and strategically select at least one MAINLY goal this month that supports your most important results.

In the next chapter, you will learn how to write *annual goals* very powerfully using the Annual Backwards Goals form. Selecting a monthly goal to support a desired annual goal is a *strategic* way to select montly goals.

Finally, you can review your own inventory of goal ideas using the bonus lesson called The Future Generator™ available at www.aaron .com/DoubleYourIncome.

With these five sources in mind, it will be easy for you to strategically select a goal that is totally parallel with where you wish to go in this lifetime, this year, and this month.

Using this powerful focused technique, you have assurance that your goals will line up to produce the big results you want in this lifetime, this year, and this month.

One last comment concerns the selection of goals. It is not mandatory to select goals strategically. Let me explain. Maybe you have a desire to write a book and you are contemplating recording a *Mess* goal to clean your garage. A clean garage might have nothing *directly* to do with writing a book, but it is totally allowable to select garage-cleaning as your mess goal. Not every single one of the six goals will strategically and directly support one of your desires. However, if *none* of your six goals supports your desires in any direct way, then do not expect to get what you want in this lifetime.

So, what is the compromise position? Typically, I notice that I record three to five of the six goals that are directly related to what I stated that month as my desires. The other goals are simply what I need to get done this month to move my life forward in other ways.

Selecting and Recording Your Mess Goal

A *mess* is any discrepancy between what is inside you (in your heart, your desires, etc.) versus what is outside you (what you have manifested in the physical world). Messes can be physical, like a desktop, a garage, a clothes closet, and so on. Messes can also be emotional, like a disturbing relationship, an unreturned book, an overdue apology, and so on.

You can simply think of lots of messes in your mind and then select one. That's not a bad idea, but there is a better one. A better idea is *The Future Generator*.

The Future Generator is a fascinating process of creating a warehouse of ideas from which to draw future goals. It is an *inventory* of goal ideas. It is a list of gems that are just hopes today, but that one day will rise to the level of being well-written goals.

That's one purpose of The Future Generator—to create a complete list of goal ideas so that you won't ever forget what you want. The second purpose, paradoxically, is the exact opposite: It's so that you *can* forget. Because your goal ideas are recorded in The Future Generator, you no longer have to keep them in your mind. They are on paper for your future reference.

Indeed, you will not just have a list, you will have a *categorized* listing, actually six lists, one for each of the six goal pathways. Then, each month, you simply refer to this list and effortlessly select the one goal in each goal pathway that is most appropriate for you to tackle that month.

You are now beginning to experience the beauty of a *mentored* life, an *organized* life, a *strategically planned* life.

The Future Generator is outside the scope of this book, but I want you to have this wisdom, as a gift from me. Simply go to www.aaron .com/DoubleYourIncome to download a full-color, printer-friendly copy of The Future Generator form along with complete instructions on how to correctly use it.

Strategically select a mess to eliminate based on the focused technique we just examined and The Future Generator.

For very important reasons in your life, the mess you have just selected is the most important mess to clean this month. (Or, certainly, it is one of the most important messes.)

Now you simply fill in the blanks on the MAINLY form to create a perfect goal (see Figure 9.2a and b). It is so easy when you use the MAINLY form. When you fill in the blanks you effortlessly call into action the Law of Attraction.

Select a mess. Is it your taxes, or your closet, or your car, or your desktop? Once you have chosen the mess, record the word that names or labels the mess in the blank: "I will clean the following Mess _____."

Select a date for completion of the mess goal. Remember that the deadline for this goal must be on or before the last day of the

Instructions on Completing MAINLY™ Form

 MESS

This is a circumstance in which what is outside of you is not equal to what is inside of you (incongruence). Any situation, physical thing, relationship, any aspect of your environment, or anything that you are tolerating or is not working is a Mess.

Ideas... car, closet, clothing, computer problems, debt, desktop, desk drawers, files, garage, personal issues, personal surroundings, relationship with spouse/children/co-workers, shed, taxes

 ACKNOWLEDGMENT

This is a way to show your appreciation to a person, a company or to a group of people.

Ideas... children, clients, co-workers, employees, employer, exceptional service received from someone, joint venture partners, team members, committee members, family members, partners, favor received from someone

 INCREASE IN WEALTH

This is a way to increase your income or net worth, or decrease your debts or expenses. This is where to record your money goals.

Ideas... debt reduction, financial plan, investing, getting more clients, networking, raising fees or prices, buying real estate, new sales generated in your business, improving your referral system, savings, stocks, mortgaging, selling something

 NEW

This is something new that you want to have or do, that you have not had or done before. It is a new way of doing something in your life or some new experience.

Ideas... develop a new product or service, try a new restaurant, meet new people, get updated computer software to stay current with technology, read a new book, update your wardrobe, do something you've never done before, new experiences, new place to visit, try different food, create a website, new way of doing something

 LEARN

This is something you want to learn in order to help you in your business or personal life.

Ideas... to become skilled in a particular area, learn a computer program, learn personal skills, take a course, improve in a sport or hobby, learn how to use a specific piece of equipment (i.e. camera, computer)

 YOURSELF

This is doing something just for yourself - taking care of you! Think of what you would just love to allow yourself to do or to allow yourself as a treat.

Ideas... attend a special event, eliminate addictions, exercise, fulfill childhood dream/desire, golf (or any sport you enjoy), have fun, meditation, quiet time, read, reduce fats/sugars/soft drinks, select a role model, spend time with special people in your life, spirituality, a vacation to rejuvenate, body (fitness/nutrition)

Figure 9.2a   Definitions and Examples of the six MAINLY™ Pathways

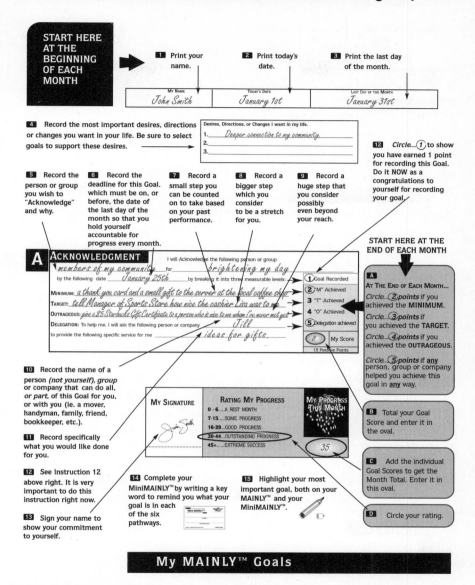

START HERE AT THE BEGINNING OF EACH MONTH

1 Print your name.

2 Print today's date.

3 Print the last day of the month.

MY NAME	TODAY'S DATE	LAST DAY OF THE MONTH
John Smith	January 1st	January 31st

4 Record the most important desires, directions or changes you want in your life. Be sure to select goals to support these desires.

Desires, Directions, or Changes I want in my life.
1. Deeper connection to my community.
2.
3.

12 Circle...① to show you have earned 1 point for recording this Goal. Do it NOW as a congratulations to yourself for recording your goal.

5 Record the person or group you wish to "Acknowledge" and why.

6 Record the deadline for this Goal, which must be on, or before, the date of the last day of the month so that you hold yourself accountable for progress every month.

7 Record a small step you can be counted on to take based on your past performance.

8 Record a bigger step which you consider to be a stretch for you.

9 Record a huge step that you consider possibly even beyond your reach.

START HERE AT THE END OF EACH MONTH

A ACKNOWLEDGMENT

members of my community   I will Acknowledge the following person or group   for   brightening my day
by the following date   January 25th   by breaking it into three measurable levels:

MINIMUM: a thank you card and a small gift to the server at the local coffee shop
TARGET: tell Manager of Sports Store how nice the cashier Lisa was to me
OUTRAGEOUS: give a $5 Starbucks Gift Certificate to a person who is nice to me whom I've never met yet
DELEGATION: To help me, I will ask the following person or company   Jill
to provide the following specific service for me   ideas for gifts.

① Goal Recorded
② "M" Achieved
3 "T" Achieved
4 "O" Achieved
⑤ Delegation achieved

8 My Score
15 Possible Points

A AT THE END OF EACH MONTH...

Circle..②points if you achieved the MINIMUM.

Circle..③points if you achieved the TARGET.

Circle..④points if you achieved the OUTRAGEOUS.

Circle..⑤points if any person, group or company helped you achieve this goal in any way.

10 Record the name of a person (not yourself), group or company that can do all, or part, of this Goal for you, or with you (ie. a mover, handyman, family, friend, bookkeeper, etc.).

11 Record specifically what you would like done for you.

12 See Instruction 12 above right. It is very important to do this instruction right now.

13 Sign your name to show your commitment to yourself.

MY SIGNATURE
John Smith

RATING MY PROGRESS
0 - 6....A REST MONTH
7-15...SOME PROGRESS
16-29...GOOD PROGRESS
30-44...OUTSTANDING PROGRESS
45+......EXTREME SUCCESS

MY PROGRESS THIS MONTH

35

B Total your Goal Score and enter it in the oval.

C Add the individual Goal Scores to get the Month Total. Enter it in this oval.

D Circle your rating.

14 Complete your MiniMAINLY™ by writing a key word to remind you what your goal is in each of the six pathways.

15 Highlight your most important goal, both on your MAINLY™ and your MiniMAINLY™.

Mini MAINLY™

My MAINLY™ Goals

Figure 9.2b   Instructions to Complete MAINLY™ Form and Completed Example

month. Why must your deadlines be within the month? The answer is very important: You want to be accountable. You want to be on a path of continually moving forward. You want to differentiate yourself from others who rarely move forward (and when they do, it is only due to outside influences and not by inner design).

Here is an example:

> I will clean the following Mess *my closet* by the following date *January 25* before the last day of the month.

You now need to break your intended goal into the three levels of challenge: Minimum, Target, and Outrageous. (This concept was explained in Chapter 7, "Achieve Your Goals for Sure.")

Think of what part of your intended goal you can be counted on to achieve—based on your past performance, not on your hopes or dreams or commitments or pride. That is your *Minimum Level*™. Record it. Do not worry that this level is too easy. It is the job of this level to ensure that you do indeed have a success, so, the easier the better.

Next, think of a stretch. Think of a bigger part of that intended goal that is beyond what you are confident you could achieve—in other words, where there is some uncertainty or some hope. As explained in Chapter 7, this is called the *Target Level*™. It may contain the Minimum Level, in which case achieving the Target means that you have automatically achieved the Minimum. One example of that would be the case where the Minimum was to discard half of the old clothes and the Target was to discard all of the old clothes. The other possibility is the case where the Target is unrelated to the Minimum except for the evaluation that the Target is more challenging to you than the Minimum. Keeping with our example, it may be more challenging for you to organize all the shoes than to discard old clothes.

The example goal now reads:

> I will clean the following Mess *my closet* by the following date *January 25* before the last day of the month, by breaking it into three measurable levels:
> **Minimum:** Discard old clothes.
> **Target:** Organize all shoes.

Now imagine an extraordinarily challenging aspect of this intended goal. Make it really Outrageous. No one will fault you if you do not achieve it, especially not in one month. Create something Outrageous so that your mind can begin working on it, even if consciously you do not.

Again using our example, you have always seen space-saving shelving in other people's homes and longed to have it in your home. You have always thought that it would never happen. You have selected this as your *Outrageous Level*™. The example goal now reads:

> I will clean the following Mess _my closet_ by the following date _January 25_ before the last day of the month, by breaking it into three measurable levels:
> **Minimum:** Discard old clothes.
> **Target:** Organize all shoes.
> **Outrageous:** Install space-saving shelving.

Delegation

It is not your job to do the goal. It is only your job to ensure that it gets done. You may be poorly equipped to complete this goal in terms of tools available, skills, time available, level of interest, disposition, pressure to get other tasks handled at the same time, and so on.

"You can achieve anything you want in life, as long as you don't care who gets the credit."
—U.S. President Ronald Reagan

There are many reasons why you might not be the right person to do this goal. Nevertheless, you are the one who wants it done. What is the solution? It's called *delegation*.

Maybe you have never delegated before. Maybe that word scares you or intimidates you. Maybe you think that only big corporate executives can delegate. Nevertheless, it is time for you to delegate. There are many ways to do it.

You could:

- Find someone to help you via the Internet, like the wonderful free service www.craigslist.org. Simply surf into that web site, select the city in which you live, and post a notice: "I want someone to install space-saving shelving in my clothes closet."

You will likely be startled both at how many people reply and also at how little they will charge you. It's fun. Try it.

- Hire someone from the *Yellow Pages* or from an ad in the newspaper.
- Retain a professional (bookkeeper, accountant, professional organizer, housekeeper, cook, etc.).
- Ask a friend or neighbor to help you.
- Ask a relative to help you.
- Offer to barter with someone, whereby that person would eliminate this mess for you (all or part of it) and you would help that person in some way that you enjoy doing and can do well.

"You set goals only in those areas where you are not competent."

—Raymond Aaron

Be creative. If you do not have much money, then ask for favors or offer to barter.

In fact, the most important part of the MAINLY form is the delegation. And the reason is fascinating.

If you regularly meditate every morning, then you would not set a goal to meditate every morning. Only those people who don't meditate and who want to begin would set such a goal. Stated in another way, you set goals only in those areas where you are not competent.

If you attempt to work as a lone-wolf, setting out to do all the work necessary to achieve every one of your goals, you are definitely embarking on a tough life. You are intentionally choosing to work in areas where you are not competent.

If you are, by definition, not competent at your own goal, then it is easy to find someone who could either do it for you or support you in getting it done. All the agonizing and efforting and procrastinating simply disappear when you find a person who is competent at it to do the goal for you or with you.

Right now you may be thinking that it is more *wholesome* to do the goal yourself. You may feel that you will learn important skills, or that you will become a better person by forcing yourself to get something done that you do not particularly enjoy doing.

"If you spend your life working on your weaknesses, at the end of your life you will have lots of strong weaknesses."

—Dan Sullivan,
The Strategic Coach™

That is a common thought. But, it is not a valuable thought. If you are not competent at a task and someone else is, then let that person do it for you while you do what you love. Everyone wins—particularly you, who gets to have a goal achieved without your own effort.

Your intent now is to think of who could do all or part of this goal with you or for you. You may think of a specific person—Sarah, Frank, or Mike. You may think of a category—neighbor, relative, bookkeeper, accountant, housekeeper, handyman, roofer, mechanic, and so on. You may know such a person or you may need to seek such a person by referral or by reading ads in the newspaper or on the Internet.

Now that you have thought of a person, think of specifically what that person could do for you to help you achieve your goal. Enter that information into your goal. In our example, you have decided to go to a local hardware store and ask for a referral of a closet organizer. Hence, the example now reads:

> I will clean the following Mess _my closet_ by the following date _January 25_ before the last day of the month, by breaking it into three measurable levels:
>   **Minimum:** Discard old clothes.
>   **Target:** Organize all shoes.
>   **Outrageous:** Install space-saving shelving.
>   **Delegation:** To help me, I will ask the following person or company _my local hardware store_ to provide the following specific service for me _recommend a closet organizer._

Not only must the goal itself be measurable, but we are actually able to measure our monthly progress using a unique scoring system embedded in the MAINLY form. You will see how powerful the scoring system is later in this chapter. For now, simply reward yourself by circling the number _1_, which is the number of points you get for simply recording a goal.

Why would you get a _goal-achieving_ point for simply _recording_ a goal? The answer to this paradox lies in the fact that just by recording a goal you take a huge step toward achieving it. Recording the goal is actually all that the Law of Attraction needs to begin achieving it for you. So take your point and enjoy it. Sometimes, scoring that one point will be all you need to do to fully achieve the goal itself.

Record the Other Five Goals on the MAINLY Form

Now, go on to the second goal—*Acknowledgment*. As with the Mess goal:

- Use the focused technique of selecting an acknowledgment goal by thinking about your loves, your Life Missions, and your three most important results, and also review your Future Generator and your Annual Backwards Goals.
- Decide on an important Acknowledgment for this month.
- Fill in the blanks on the MAINLY form.
- Decide on a delegation.
- Circle number *1* to reward yourself for writing an Acknowledgment goal.

Do the *Increase in Wealth* goal, the *New* goal, and the *Learn* goal. Finally, select a goal just for *Yourself*, for this month. Then *sign* the MAINLY form as a commitment to yourself.

The next step is a fascinating one that strongly invokes the wonderful Law of Attraction. Review your six goals and select the one goal that is most important. In other words, if you totally failed in five goals and yet achieved Outrageous in one goal, which one goal would you most want that to be? Once you have selected that most important goal, take a highlighter and neatly highlight that entire goal. This draws attention and energy to that goal, which strongly calls the Law of Attraction into play.

The MAINLY Form

Unfortunately, many Monthly Mentor members simply file the completed MAINLY form and do not look at it until the end of the month, when it is time to score successes. This process does not support well the Law of Attraction. Yet, it is awkward to carry around the MAINLY form. What is the solution?

The solution is a wallet-sized card called the *MiniMAINLY* ™ form. (See Figure 9.3 for a MiniMAINLY blank form and Figure 9.4 for a completed MiniMAINLY form.) You can photocopy it from Figure 9.3, or you can download it from www.aaron.com/DoubleYourIncome.

Cut on the dotted lines and paste the front and the back together. You now have a wallet-sized card. The front of the MiniMAINLY card asks you to fill in your name and the last day of the month. Turn over the card, and there you will find six boxes, one for each

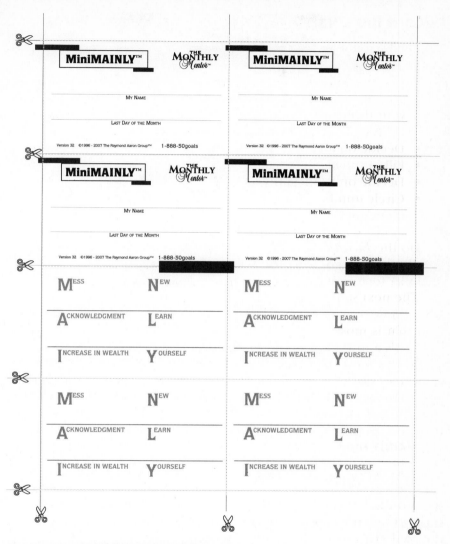

Figure 9.3   MiniMAINLY™ Blank Form

of the six MAINLY pathways of life. Record a keyword to remind you of the goal you recorded on the MAINLY form. For example, in the Mess cell, you would record simply, "My Closet."

Next, highlight the same goal on the MiniMAINLY as you did on the MAINLY form. Now, what should you do with this completed MiniMAINLY?

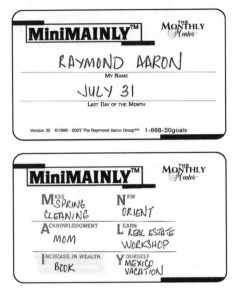

Figure 9.4 Completed Mini Mainly Form

Carry the MiniMAINLY with you in your wallet, possibly in front of your credit card or ATM card, so you see it frequently throughout the month. Put it on your mirror at home. Basically, place it where you will see it. It will act as a constant reminder, which is an important part of calling the powerful Law of Attraction into play.

That's the complete MAINLY process. *Bravo!* You are now on the path to achieving your six goals every month, and having the Universe do some of the work for you through employing the Law of Attraction.

During the Month Make a notation in your calendar to review your goals weekly and to grade yourself at the end of the month. Actually schedule time to work on and achieve your goals. The more energy you put into your goals, the more work the Universe will do also.

Measurable Monthly Progress at the End of the Month This is the most wonderful part of faithfully recording goals. You get to have hard evidence of your progress.

At month-end, take that month's MAINLY form and score yourself on your progress. You already have one point for recording each goal. Give yourself another 2 points if you achieved Minimum. Give yourself another 3 points if you achieved Target, regardless of whether you achieved Minimum. Give yourself another 4 points if you achieved Outrageous, regardless of whether you achieved Minimum or Target.

Give yourself 5 points if *any* person, computer program, service, web site, group, or company helped you in *any* way to achieve *any* part of your goal. Delegation points are not rewarded *just* for using the person you thought of and recorded at the beginning of the month. You are allowed to be flexible during the month and uncover *any* worthwhile way to get help in achieving your goal.

Total your goal score. It is out of 15 maximum. If you recorded your goal at the beginning of the month, then your goal total will be between 1 and 15.

Now, sum all your six goal totals to get a monthly total. That number itself is not of interest. But, what it means is of great interest. Look up your monthly total on the table on the MAINLY form, as shown here:

1–6	A rest month
7–15	Some progress
16–29	Good progress
30–44	Outstanding progress
Over 44	Extreme success

Enjoy your rating of progress. If it is low, appreciate what you did do and make a firm commitment to do better next month. If you did well, keep it up. Bask in the joy of the achievements.

FAQs

1. **Are the ratings of progress too lenient?**
   You might wonder why getting just seven points, for example, is considered "some progress" when all you need to do is record six goals and achieve one Minimum. Here is the answer. What I have found in mentoring thousands of members is that some months it will be a success for you just to be playing the game. Just recording your goals means that you are intent on moving forward even if life got in the way that month.

Keep in mind that achieving a Minimum Level goal is, of course, very easy. But, achieving six of them is not so easy.

Also, keep in mind that the score that most people on this planet would attain each month would be *zero*. You are in an elite group, even just recording your goals and achieving them to the Minimum.

Finally, remember the lesson that Aesop taught you in his wonderful parable, "The Tortoise and the Hare." He taught you that the tortoise always beats the hare. In Monthly Mentor terms, you will go much further in your life if you consistently achieve even your Minimums versus some months hitting an occasional Outrageous. Keep hitting even just your Minimums and your life will move strategically in the direction of your choice.

2. **What is the procedure for a goal that needs far more than a month to attain?**
   Record, as your goal this month, the *part* of the big goal that might be achievable this month. For example, if you want to pass a big exam several months from now, you may record how much studying you will do this month or how many books you will read or how you will do on an upcoming test this month. In the next chapter, "Annual Backwards Goals," you will be introduced to a unique way of recording those big goals you wish to achieve but that require more than a month.

3. **Is there one more little secret that has not been shared yet?**
   Yes. I have noticed that recording goals *neatly* gives you a greater chance for success. I think it is the psychological issue that taking the patience and attention to record your goals neatly and clearly sets those goals more firmly in your mind. It proves to your subconscious that you are serious. And it alerts the universal Law of Attraction that you are placing lots of energy into this goal so it better get working to achieve it for you.

Three Expert Action Steps

You know all the rules for recording goals properly and you have put them together in this powerful chapter. You know the six pathways of life and you have followed them in this chapter to record your six goals. You got an extra bonus from learning an additional lesson at www.aaron.com/DoubleYourIncome. You learned how to strategically choose your goals. You know how to subdivide your goals into the three levels. You learned the beauty of delegation and got points for it in this chapter. You learned how to score your progress so that you could enjoy measurable monthly progress. And you know that you can get copies of MAINLY and MiniMAINLY at www.aaron.com/DoubleYourIncome.

It is time to use what you have learned. Below are listed the Three Expert Action Steps™ designed to support you in bringing what you have just read into play in your life. Once you have completed these Three Expert Action Steps, you will be ready to move on to the next chapter, which introduces you to a concept of recording those great big annual goals you desire, as if they are already achieved. You will learn to write goals backwards!

> **First Expert Action Step: Record your six MAINLY goals using the focused technique.**
> Review the whole chapter carefully and record your goals on this fill-in-the-blanks form, remembering, of course, to mark your most important goal with a highlighter and to circle *1* to get your goal-recording point.

> **Second Expert Action Step: Complete your accompanying Mini-MAINLY card.**
> Complete this card and carry it with you or put it where you will see it regularly. Remember to highlight the same goal on the MiniMAINLY that you did on the MAINLY.

> **Third Expert Action Step: Calendar your next steps.**
> Make an entry in your calendar to review your goals weekly. Make an entry in your calendar to evaluate your progress on the last day of the month.

Moving On

Now you have earned the right to read the next chapter, where you will learn how to realize your significant goals for the year—and why you should record them backwards!

10

Annual Backwards Goals

HOW YOU CAN MOVE STRATEGICALLY TOWARD REALIZING EVEN YOUR BIGGEST GOALS

Where do you envision yourself at the end of the year? What will you have achieved? Who will you be? How do you ensure your monthly goals line up with your vision for the year?

Strategic versus Tactical

What is the difference between strategic and tactical action?

Strategic relates to taking action with the end in mind—to having an overall vision. It involves understanding the project as a whole, and doing those things that facilitate the overall end result.

Tactical relates to taking those short-term actions along the way that support the strategic end result.

How does this apply to goal-setting?

In the previous chapter, you learned how to record six monthly goals for each of the six pathways on the MAINLY™ form. But are those goals strategic or tactical? Considering they are one-month goals, they have to fall into the category of "tactical." Typically, strategic goals, strategic plans, strategic planning, and strategic thinking are longer term. So, anything that's one month long is tactical.

Are your tactical monthly goals lined up with your overall strategy as to where you want to be a year from now? Maybe they are, and maybe they're not. Would you like a way to make sure that they are lined up? One way is by recording *annual goals*; that's a strategic task. It's saying, "This is what I want to produce in a year"; so doing your annual goals is an inherently strategic plan.

Writing Goals Backwards

I teach my Monthly Mentor™ members to write their yearly goals backwards. Let me explain.

Once something's been done, it's easier to do it the second time. I know you've heard the joke, "The second million is easier than the first, so I'm just going to start on my second million." It's a joke, but as with all humor, there's an element of truth. What is the truth in it? The truth is that it is easier to do something when you have already done it before.

The fascinating point to make here is that your mind cannot tell whether you have done it or whether you just *say* you have done it. If you say you've done it and record it on paper, your mind acts as if you have already done it. This means it's easier to do it the "second" time. If your mind thinks it's doing it a second time, but you're body is actually only doing it the first time, somehow it is easier to do it because your mind thinks it is easier. Let's use every possible benefit and advantage in order to allow us to get our goals achieved more easily.

John Landy and Dr. Roger Bannister tried unsuccessfully for years to break the infamous four-minute mile. Finally, one day Roger Bannister broke the record. Everyone knew that the next time Landy were to run a mile race he would break the four-minute mile, because it had already been done. John Landy was in Australia, and Roger Bannister was in England. They were 12 time zones apart on opposite sides of the world in opposite hemispheres, and yet, everybody knew Landy would do it. And, everyone was right. In his very next mile race, Landy indeed broke four minutes and also broke Bannister's new world record.

> *"Picture yourself in your mind's eye as having already achieved this goal. See yourself doing the things you'll be doing when you've reached your goal."*
>
> —Earl Nightingale

The twofold purpose of the exercise in this chapter is, first, for you to have written annual goals so that you focus your monthly efforts toward your annual goals. When you just write MAINLY goals without an overview, that's fine. You achieve quite a bit each month, but it's far more powerful for your MAINLY goals to serve your annual interests.

The second purpose is to record goals as if you've already achieved them. This is the unique way in which you record annual goals in The Monthly Mentor program. You record goals as if they're already achieved so that your mind thinks they're already done, making it easier to actually achieve them "the second time."

In order to plant the seed in your mind that you have already achieved the goal, you are going to do something quite unusual. Instead of imagining that you are at the beginning of the year setting goals for the end of the year, you're going to pretend the whole year is already over and you are looking back on the year and congratulating yourself on your wonderful successes.

"I couldn't wait for success, so I went ahead without it."

—Jonathan Winters

Why is that important?

First, if you are congratulating yourself for having done it, then your mind thinks you've done it; therefore, it's easier to do it the second time. Planting that thought firmly in your mind is yet another way you invoke the wonderful Law of Attraction.

There's another advantage. Say you desire to record a really big goal, like having an income 10 times higher than you have ever had before. Though that may inspire you, it more likely will seem oppressive to your mind because it is just so gigantic. So, when you're looking *forward* at a huge goal, it might feel heavy. When you're looking back and saying, "Congratulations—I increased my income by ten times," the bigger the better, because you're celebrating your success.

The interesting thing is that sometimes just recording an outrageous goal is all you need to do in order to achieve it. So many of my mentored clients say to me, "I wrote a goal that was so wildly outrageous I didn't think it could ever possibly be done, and here it is halfway through the year and I've already done it. How is that possible?" It is possible because you wrote it down. You wrote it down *in the past tense.* You congratulated yourself for doing it; your mind thought it had already been done, so doing it a second time was not such a big deal.

You are now going to complete your annual goals for the remainder of this year. Where do you obtain the special form?

- You can photocopy the forms from this chapter. (Note that because of the size of the pages of this book, the forms are presented smaller than the actual ones.)
- You can go to www.aaron.com/DoubleYourIncome to obtain printer-friendly versions of the two forms needed for the Annual Backwards Goals™ process.

Congratulating Yourself for Your Successes

You'll notice there are two different forms that are part of the Annual Backwards Goals process.

The first form is entitled *Front Page* (Letter to "You of Last Year"). You are now going to complete the first form. (See Figure 10.1.)

Record today's date, and that is actually the date if you look at a calendar today. The reason I say that is because you are going to be using another date as well. You're going to be using, inside the letter, the last day of the year that you're writing the goal for. No matter what today's date actually is, inside the letter the date is December 31 of the planning year.

Next, record your name where it says "My Name."

Let me now review the important parts of your letter for you.

Dear Raymond, who lived through last year for me . . .

Of course, last year is the year for which you're planning, the year that you're really at the beginning of, but you're tricking your mind into thinking that you are at the end of it.

As I review the past, I thank you for living through such an important year for me. Your successes . . .

Notice you are calling them *successes* so your mind thinks you've done them.

Your successes will now allow me to enter the coming New Year without the drain of problems hanging over from the past. Some successes were difficult for you, requiring skill, concentration, planning, and effort. In particular, I noticed you used your skills of _____ . . .

ANNUAL BACKWARDS GOALS™
NEXT YEAR'S GOALS, AS IF ALREADY ACHIEVED

THE MONTHLY Mentor™

FRONT PAGE

PURPOSE: **BENEFITS:**

• To have written Annual Goals	**so that you** . . . . . . focus your monthly efforts toward your Annual Goals.
• To record Goals, as if already achieved	**so that your** . . . . . . mind thinks they are already done, making them easier to achieve.

_____
① TODAY'S DATE

LETTER TO "YOU OF LAST YEAR"

December 31ˢᵗ, 20___
② GOAL YEAR END DATE

Dear_____, who lived through last year for me:
③ MY NAME

As I review the past, I thank you for living through such an important year for me. Your successes will now allow me to enter the coming New Year, without the drain of problems hanging over from the past.

Some successes were difficult for you, requiring skill, concentration, planning and effort. In particular, I noticed you used your skills of...

④ _____
_____
_____

Wonderfully, though, some of the seemingly toughest successes occurred almost effortlessly!

Also, you ensured that your Goals supported our Loves by linking each Goal to the Love(s) it supported so that you knew why you wanted to achieve each

Goal. Also, it ensured that you did not inadvertently waste a year by forgetting to move closer to one of our listed Loves.

In particular, I acknowledge and congratulate you especially for...
⑤ _____
_____
_____.

Thank you again.
Love,

_____
⑥ MY SIGNATURE

Figure 10.1   Annual Backwards Goals Blank Front Page Letter

Record the skills that you had to use, the skills that you were most proud of using in order to accomplish the successes that you've achieved. You can record whatever skills you had to call into play in order to achieve your wonderful successes. Obviously, you do not know what skills will have been, in fact, required at this point in time. Just imagine what skills you would desire and record them.

> Wonderfully, though, some of the seemingly toughest "successes" occurred almost effortlessly.

By writing this, some of your successes will actually achieve themselves effortlessly just because you wrote it, just because you planted that seed, just because you set that wheel in motion. This is the Law of Attraction.

> Also, you ensured that your Goals supported our Loves by linking each Goal to the Love it supported so that you knew why you wanted to achieve each Goal. Also, it ensured that you did not inadvertently waste a year by forgetting to move closer to one of our listed Loves.

How often do people say, "I love my grandchildren, but I haven't seen them in a year." "I love reading, but I haven't read much since I left school." "I like to exercise, but it's been a few years." People talk about things they love and then bemoan the fact they haven't done them for years. It is because they haven't set goals and planned for them. What you're going to be doing is linking each of your goals (successes) to the love that it supports so that you have a reason for doing it. When it's near the end of the year and you haven't fully achieved a particular goal, seeing the love it would support will give you additional desire to complete the goal. This, too, invokes the Law of Attraction by adding a strong dose of emotion to the intellectual task of recording goals.

> In particular, I acknowledge and congratulate you especially for . . .

Record one or two goals that you're most proud that you achieved. This isn't actually where you record a goal. It is just where you complement yourself for some big thing you did. It's just to highlight a very important goal. You're actually going to record your goals on another sheet of paper, but this is simply to highlight one or two of them.

> Thank you again.

Here you give love to yourself by signing your name.

Now, with this page done, your mind is set that it's December 31. Imagine that in a few hours you have to shower for your New Year's party. Put in your mind that Santa Claus has already come and gone, that this is the end of the year, and you're looking back over the year.

Your next job is to write your actual annual goals. You're going to think of them as *successes*; therefore, you have to write them in the past tense.

Getting Ready to Record Your Annual Goals

As explained before, you may get printer-friendly copies of the Goal Page from www.aaron.com/DoubleYourIncome. (See Figure 10.2.)

You'll notice the Goal Page has three identical templates for you to record goals. You can print on the front and back of the sheet of paper so that each sheet will then have six templates. Or, just print on the front and have three templates per sheet. You will need to have *six* such identical Goal Pages in front of you; one for each of the six goal pathways.

You must now get each of the six Goal Pages ready for use.

At the top of the page it says *Goal Page for* _____, and here's where you print in your name. For the year 200_, write in the year that you're recording your goals for.

You will notice a circled *7*. I want you to circle "M = Mess" because this is going to be the page on which you record your Mess goals, or, more correctly, your Mess successes.

Slightly lower down, where it says *Annual Goal number*, you'll see there is a circled *8*; I want you to write in the number "M1": *M* for "Mess" and the number *1* since this will be your first annual Mess goal.

In the second template on the page, you write "M2" (for your second annual mess goal). Similarly, in the bottom template on the page, you write "M3" (for your third annual Mess goal). If you choose to have more than three Mess goals for this year, turn the page over and record "M4," "M5," and "M6." Indeed, to have more than six Mess goals accomplished this year, simply continue this process using as many pages as you wish.

What is the correct number of goals that you should have in the Mess category or in any of the six categories? The answer is: It depends on you. You might have just one Mess goal, one big mess that you want to clean up, or you might have 10. It's up to you.

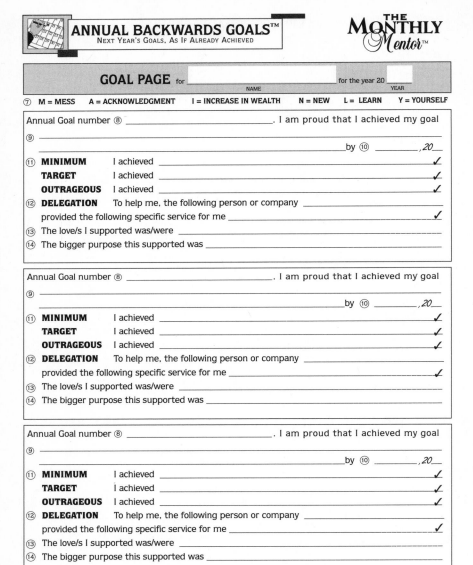

Figure 10.2 Annual Backwards Goals Completed Front Page Letter

One year, you might be focusing on increasing your wealth; therefore, you might have numerous "Increase in Wealth" goals for that year.

Now, take the next identical form, also entitled, *Goal Page*. (See Figure 10.3.) Record your name and the same year and circle

```
┌──────────────────────────────┐
│          GOAL PAGE           │
└──────────────────────────────┘
```

⑦ M = MESS   A = ACKNOWLEDGMENT   I = INCREASE IN WEALTH   N = NEW   L = LEARN   Y = YOURSELF

Annual Goal number ⑧ _____. I am proud that I achieved my goal

⑨ _____

_____by ⑩ _____ , 20___

⑪ **MINIMUM**   I achieved _____ ✓

    TARGET   I achieved _____ ✓

    OUTRAGEOUS   I achieved _____ ✓

⑫ **DELEGATION**   To help me, the following person or company _____

provided the following specific service for me _____ ✓

⑬ The love/s I supported was/were _____

⑭ The bigger purpose this supported was _____

Annual Goal number ⑧ _____. I am proud that I achieved my goal

⑨ _____

_____by ⑩ _____ , 20___

⑪ **MINIMUM**   I achieved _____ ✓

    TARGET   I achieved _____ ✓

    OUTRAGEOUS   I achieved _____ ✓

⑫ **DELEGATION**   To help me, the following person or company _____

provided the following specific service for me _____ ✓

⑬ The love/s I supported was/were _____

⑭ The bigger purpose this supported was _____

Annual Goal number ⑧ _____. I am proud that I achieved my goal

⑨ _____

_____by ⑩ _____ , 20___

⑪ **MINIMUM**   I achieved _____ ✓

    TARGET   I achieved _____ ✓

    OUTRAGEOUS   I achieved _____ ✓

⑫ **DELEGATION**   To help me, the following person or company _____

provided the following specific service for me _____ ✓

⑬ The love/s I supported was/were _____

⑭ The bigger purpose this supported was _____

Figure 10.3   Blank Annual Backwards Goals Page

"A = Acknowledgment," and down the page write "A1," "A2," and "A3." You can write on the back if you wish and record "A4," "A5," and "A6," but please don't imagine that you need to do exactly three or six or that you're not good enough if you don't have six. You record as many or as few as you wish.

Please Follow These INSTRUCTIONS:

A. The concept is that you imagine you are already at the end of the upcoming year (which we call the Goal Year), thinking back about your successes. Of course, in the "real" situation, you are situated here today at the beginning of the upcoming Goal Year looking forward, wondering if you will be able to achieve your goals. It is better to be proud of your achievements than to be wondering if you will have any.

B. Print ① Today's Date and ③ Your Name.

C. Think of the upcoming Goal Year, for which you will soon be recording your Annual Backwards Goals™. Record the ② Goal Year End Date.

D. You have now begun writing a letter to yourself. More accurately, it is a letter to the "you" who lived through the Goal Year for you, as if it has already occurred. Read the letter. It is your letter.

④ Record some skills you needed to achieve your goals.

⑤ Record what you are (or will be) most proud of achieving.

⑥ Sign your letter to yourself. Now that your letter is written, it is time to record the goals for which you just congratulated yourself. Use the Annual Backwards Goals™ **GOAL PAGE** form, to record your Goals.

⑦ Circle the appropriate goal pathway this goal relates to: M=Mess, A=Acknowledgment, I=Increase In Wealth, N=New, L=Learn, and Y=Yourself.

⑧ Record the first letter of the appropriate goal pathway along with the number of your Annual Backwards Goals™. For example: M1, M2, M3, ... ,A1, A2, A3, ...

⑨ Record your Goal.

⑩ Record the date for completion of this Goal, which must be within the Goal Year.

⑪ Divide the Goal into three levels—Minimum, Target, and Outrageous. Record the three levels of the Goal.

⑫ Record the name of a person, group, or company that can do all, or part, of this Goal for you, or with you (i.e., a mover, handyman, bookkeeper, etc.).

⑬ Record the love/s you are supporting through attaining this goal.

⑭ Record the bigger purpose of achieving this goal.

⑮ During the Goal Year, check (✓) each Goal as it is achieved.

SAMPLE: *November 16ᵗʰ, 2006*
① TODAY'S DATE

December 31ˢᵗ, 2007
② GOAL YEAR END DATE

Dear *John Smith* , who lived through last year for me:
③ MY NAME

As I review the past, I thank you for living through such an important year for me. Your successes will now allow me to enter the coming New Year, without the drain of problems hanging over from the past.

Some successes were difficult for you, requiring skill, concentration, planning and effort. In particular, I noticed you used your skills of ④ *patience, kindness and open-heartedness* .

In particular, I acknowledge and congratulate you especially for ⑤ *applying your wonderful skills which have worked so well for you in the past in other areas of your life to these new areas* .

Thank you again. Love,   *John Smith*
⑥ MY SIGNATURE

⑦ M = MESS   A = ACKNOWLEDGMENT   I = INCREASE IN WEALTH   N = NEW   L = LEARN   (Y = YOURSELF)

Annual Goal number ⑧ *Y1* . I am proud that I achieved my goal

⑨ *weight control*
by ⑩ *September 18, 20 07*

⑪ **MINIMUM**   I achieved *weighing at most 190 pounds*
  TARGET   I achieved *weighing at most 180 pounds*
  OUTRAGEOUS I achieved *weighing at most 170 pounds*

⑫ **DELEGATION**   To help me, the following person or company *weight loss coach*
provided the following specific service for me *personalized plan*

⑬ The love/s I supported was/were *being healthy and fit*

⑭ The bigger purpose this supported was *great dad*

Figure 10.4   Blank Annual Backwards Goal Page 2

Then, on the next sheet of paper, circle "I = Increase in Wealth" and do "I1," "I2," and so on, and then do this for the "N" page and the "L" page and the "Y" page.

When that's finished, you will have in front of you one letter, which is the Front Page (Letter to "You of Last Year"), and six Goal Pages, which have just little bits of information on them like your name, the year, the selection of goal pathway, and the numbering—"M1," "M2," "M3," and so on. (See Figure 10.4 for a completed example.)

You are now ready to select and record your annual goals.

Selecting and Recording Your Annual Goals

I have a magic wand and I am waving it for you. There is something I know you would just love to have improved in your life. What is it? Just say it.

What big mess would you really love to have eliminated?

"Never look down to test the ground before taking your next step; only he who keeps his eye fixed on the far horizon will find his right road."

—Dag Hammarskjold

Record the name of that goal after "I am proud that I achieved my goal." For example, you may record: *my garage* or *my relationship with John* or *my medical condition*, or whatever you perceive to be a mess.

As you think of more messes, record them under "M2," "M3," and so forth.

Note that you are not completing the entire wording of the goal; you are simply capturing and recording the names of the goals you wish to accomplish. Why? Because it is better to have the ideas captured. You then go back and fill in the details of the goals as the next step.

What works best for me is that all six pages are in front of me and then I imagine the wand is waved and I say, "Oh, my gosh, that garage is such a mess I can't stand it." Under "M1," I'll write *my garage* and then that will remind me of something else. "If my garage were clean, I could drive a new car in there. I've been holding off buying a new car because I'm unable to drive it into the garage and I want it to be protected." Maybe that's the first new car you're ever buying in your life, so you might record it under *New*. Maybe it's under *Y*, doing something just for yourself. In other words, the thought of the garage might trigger the thinking of buying a new car and so you would flip to the appropriate page, which could be the "Y" page or the "N" page, and you would record the goal title *new car* as "Y1" or "N1." Just let the ideas flow.

Remember that you're not recording monthly goals. You're recording goals that will take typically 3 to 12 months to get done. These are big goals.

Go through this contemplative process, capturing goal after goal after goal. Make sure you have at least one, and hopefully at least three, goals in each goal pathway. You will find this exciting because you are technically *prerecording* your successes. So, the more the better and the bigger the better. Go for it—enjoy this process.

You'll notice that instruction #10 is the date. You can jam every one of your goal deadlines right up against December 31, but I don't recommend it for several reasons. One reason is you're going to have other things to do on December 31, like showering and getting ready for your New Year's party. Are you really going to want to lose weight, stop smoking, clean the garage, buy a new car, and all those other things all on the last day of the year? I don't think so.

There is another reason. You might want to paint your fence, for example, which is typically a summertime or maybe an autumn job. It's probably not a December-time job, so choose a deadline that's actually appropriate to the activity that you want to achieve.

Instruction #11 is MTO™ (Minimum, Target, Outrageous). You'll remember MTO from Chapter 7, "Achieve Your Goals for Sure":

- *Minimum* is what you can be counted on to do based on your past performance. It's not something you strive for; it's something you can be counted on to do because that's what guarantees your success.
- *Target* is typically what you think of as a goal; it's a stretch.
- *Outrageous* is what you think is way beyond your ability.

You always break goals into those three categories.

Item #12 is Delegation and it says, "to help me, the following person or company (you fill in the blank) provided the following specific service for me."

Notice that *provided* is in the past tense and notice in Minimum, Target, and Outrageous that *achieved* is in the past tense. You do not record, *I achieved will lose weight;* it doesn't even make sense grammatically. Use the past tense because you're congratulating yourself for an accomplishment that you have already had. You would, for example, correctly record: *I achieved owning the car.*

Delegation is allowing somebody else to support you in some way doing all or part of the task for you. For example, you may want to read a book, yet you can't imagine how you could ever delegate it. If you're living with somebody, you might ask your spouse, "I would like to read a book two hours a week, Monday night and Thursday night from 10:00 P.M. to 11:00 P.M. Can you support me in doing that?" If your spouse says, "Yes," then what your spouse might do for you is to remind you at 9:30 P.M. on Monday and Thursday that you want to start reading in half an hour. This will be your cue to get ready, get your pajamas on, make some tea, and ensconce yourself in your favorite chair. Your spouse would take care of the kids; make sure the television is off; answer the phone if it rings; and all those duties so that a container is created for you within which it is easy to read. Many people complain that they can't read, but they don't mean they're illiterate. What they mean is that they don't get around to it. You're not actually delegating the physical task of reading; you're delegating getting around to reading and staying seated by having your spouse take care of all of the other issues for you. Of course, you reciprocate. You could do some other tasks for your spouse. There are lots of other creative ways you can delegate all or part.

Instruction #13 is the "Loves I supported were . . ." and it might be just one love. If you cleaned your garage, maybe the love it supported was orderliness, or you love when you fulfill your promise. Whatever it is for you, record the feeling, the love that it supported.

Instruction #14 is the "bigger purpose this supported was. . . ." This may relate to the exercise My Life Missions™. Maybe your bigger purpose is a better relationship with your spouse because your spouse is unhappy that the garage is so messy. In other words, think of some bigger purpose that is the reason you're doing it.

That is what each individual goal looks like. You are almost done. It is time now to review all your goals.

I notice, right after I write my own goals, that I want to make adjustments and changes once I see all my goals recorded. I sometimes combine two goals into one, or I sometimes separate one very big goal into two goals.

Here is an example. Let's say you recorded a goal, "M1," to clean a mess in your closet, another goal, "M3," to clean a mess in your garage, and yet a third goal to clean your basement. You originally recorded three goals. In review, you thought that it would be better to create one goal called "Clean household messes" with cleaning the closet as the Minimum, cleaning the garage as the Target, and cleaning the basement as the Outrageous. This new goal would replace the other three.

Alternatively, you may have an Acknowledgment goal, "A3," to thank your family members for being so loving and supportive. Once all your annual goals are complete and you are rereading them, you may realize you would prefer to concentrate on *each* family member as an individual, deserving unique MTO levels of acknowledging. So you may abandon goal "A3" and create several new "A" goals, one for each family member.

During the Year

> *"When you determine what you want, you have made the most important decision in your life. You have to know what you want in order to attain it."*
>
> —Douglas Lurtan

Now that you have completed your Annual Backwards Goals, what do you do with them?

Keep them in a place where you will see them. Record in your calendar on the first day of each month *Look at Annual Backwards Goals*. The more your goals are in front of you, the better it is for you; that's the power of the Annual Backwards Goals. That's how to invoke the Law of Attraction.

How is the Annual Backwards Goals process a unique way to record your strategic goals?

- It's unique because you look at your goals backwards, thinking that you've already done them, making it easier to achieve them the "second time."
- It's unique because it has the patented MTO way of writing goals where you divide a goal into Minimum, Target, and Outrageous levels.
- It's unique because it divides your goals into the six MAINLY pathways of life.
- It's unique because it requires a delegation for every goal.

This is a powerful program. When you organize your thinking to divide your goals into the six pathways, when you record your goals in the backwards way, when you MTO your goals, when you delegate, and when you invoke the Law of Attraction, your goals really come true.

FAQs

1. **How long does it take to record my Annual Backwards Goals?**
   Annual Backwards Goals can take as little as one hour, but usually much longer. Set aside several hours, because when you plan your entire year really well, especially writing goals in this unique Annual Backwards Goals way, you'll be shocked to find how your life turns out the way you imagined it.

2. **What if I review my Annual Backwards Goals midway through the year and find that a particular goal is not right for me now? Do I cross it off? Do I continue to go for it?**
   Why strive for a goal that no longer holds true for you? Events will occur in your life through the year. You may change jobs, get married, get divorced, have a baby, or open a new business. At the time you record your goals, you are *the you at that point in time.* You will change and evolve through the year. Different things will happen within the year that will have an impact on you, thereby shifting your focus. Also, you may attain the Minimum of a particular goal and find that it no longer rings true for you. For example, why go for the Target, if through experiencing the Minimum of taking a golf lesson you discover you don't like golf? Give yourself permission to let go of the goal, knowing that you have now experienced it and will not go into your final days wishing that you had learned to play golf. Basically, set it up so that you win. When a goal is no longer valid, I just mark it "done" and go on.

3. **What about modifying goals throughout the year? Can I change them through the year?**
   Absolutely, yes. Change your goals if they are no longer valid. Let yourself win. Do not hold yourself to goals that no longer apply.

4. **What about 5- and 10-year goals? Other goal-setting programs cover this. Am I missing something?**
   Each different goal program offered by a different goal guru creates its own distinctions. In The Monthly Mentor, we record goals for the month (the MAINLY goals), for the year

(the Annual Backwards Goals), and for your lifetime (My Life Missions). Those three distinctions have served me and my mentored clients around the world very well.

5. **What if I'm reading this book and it's April? Do I wait till the end of the year to record my Annual Backwards Goals for the next year?**

Record your Annual Backwards Goals today! Keep in mind that you will not have the full 12 months to complete your goals. Just record them from today to the end of this year. If you are reading this and it is the latter part of the year (November), you can get a jump start and record your goals for the coming year now.

Three Expert Action Steps

You know the difference between *strategic* (Annual Backwards Goals) and *tactical* (MAINLY) goals. You know how to record your annual goals backwards since it is easier to do something the second time. You have learned that you need to link your loves and your bigger purpose to your annual goals so that you know why you want to achieve these goals. You have learned that by recording goals, some will occur automagically, through invoking the Law of Attraction.

It is time to use what you have learned. Below are listed the Three Expert Action Steps™ designed to support you in bringing what you have just read into play in your life. Once you have completed these Three Expert Action Steps, you will be ready to move on to the final chapter: "The Beginning."

First Expert Action Step

To complete the Annual Backwards Goals, either photocopy the two forms in this chapter or download a full-page, full-color, printer-friendly form from www.aaron.com/DoubleYourIncome. Complete the Front Page (Letter to "You of Last Year") using the instructions of this chapter as your guide.

Second Expert Action Step

Complete the Goal Page for each of the six goal pathways using the instructions of this chapter as your guide. For each MAINLY pathway, record at least one goal, and typically three to six (or more).

Third Expert Action Step

Make an entry in your calendar on the first day of each month to review your Annual Backwards Goals.

Moving On

Congratulations. You have your strategic plan in place for the year and for your life! The next chapter actually *launches* you into your new life.

11

The Beginning

HOW YOU CAN ENSURE YOU ACHIEVE THE SUCCESS YOU DESIRE FOR THE REST OF YOUR MENTORED LIFE

You are now at the *beginning* of your new, mentored, strategically organized life.

Leaving the Old Unmentored Life

Notice that, in an unmentored life, you know to great precision all those facts that do not matter. You know exactly when you rise in the morning. You know exactly how long it takes to get to work. You know exactly when your favorite TV show is aired each week.

But, if I had asked you, before you read this book, for your most important goals, it is likely you would not have known. They certainly would not have been neatly recorded and up to date. If I had asked if you had written goals in all areas of your life, likely you would have had to admit to me that you had no written goals at all. If I had asked how you were doing in achieving the goals of your life, you would have had no idea. If I had asked whether you wanted to employ the Law of Attraction, likely you would have wanted to, but you would not have known how to do it. If I had asked which of your loves you were fully experiencing, you would have had no idea.

If your little daughter wants to learn ballet, you find a class with a teacher. If your son wants to learn hockey, you find a team with a great coach. If one of your children doesn't do well in math, you find a tutor. In other words, you find opportunities for your children where they can be well mentored in sports, in Scouts, in Brownies, in music, in dance, and in their education. *You* also need that same mentoring. But, most adults do not seek such help for themselves and so they are forced to remain in their unmentored life.

If you think back to your education, you probably had many teachers, and yet you remember with fondness your one favorite. Imagine if every one of your teachers were as wonderful as that one teacher. Imagine what a different life you would currently have.

An unmentored life is about the *dailyness* of life. You do most chores by yourself. You spend your day attending to the tiny details of your life. As a result, tomorrow is quite the same as today. Nothing much changes; life is reasonable. Life is a to-do list.

> *"Most men lead lives of quiet desperation and go to their grave with their song still in them."*
> —Henry David Thoreau

Unfortunately, most people hope for more but settle for less. The reason is that they have not been introduced to the joys of a mentored life. This is now your chance. This is your beginning.

In summary, an unmentored life is one that simply stumbles forward in a somewhat haphazard way. There are achievements, but mostly they occur just because they occur, and not necessarily because they were well planned. You now have the tools to create a *designed* life, a strategically organized life, a life that delivers to you what you want and calls the Universe into play to deliver through the Law of Attraction so many wonderful benefits, seemingly without effort on your part.

Your New Mentored Life

You have earned the right to enjoy a mentored life. You can get considerably more detail on exactly how at www.aaron.com/DoubleYourIncome. My many mentored clients around the world are enjoying all those benefits and are grateful that they shrugged off the undirected, unmentored life of their past.

You have learned a lot in the preceding chapters. Now it's time to pull it all together and begin your journey. Remember that it is a journey, so enjoy the ride!

As you move closer and closer to what you love, you will feel more joy. You'll be pulled by a higher vision of your life, your higher purpose. You will start asking yourself important

"When you dance, your purpose is not to get to a certain place on the floor. It's to enjoy each step along the way."
—Dr. Wayne Dyer

questions. You will start making some important decisions in order to move forward. You will begin reaping the rewards of your efforts.

Once I had a dream to ride a unicycle. I didn't do anything about it for 30 years, from age 18 to age 48, and then one day I said, "This is ridiculous," and I got a coach to teach me how to

"What you get by achieving your goals is not as important as what you become by achieving your goals."
—Zig Ziglar

ride a unicycle. Now I can ride a unicycle.

On a more serious note, I wanted to get rich in real estate, so I found a mentor who was rich in real estate and who could teach it. I became a multimillionaire in real estate.

I wanted to become a great teacher and professional speaker. I found a great speaker and she taught me how to be a master in that area.

I wanted to clean my garage, so I found a very neat and organized person who swept through my chaotic garage in one weekend morning and totally cleaned and organized it.

When you set a goal, you likely wonder when you are ever going to find time to complete it. When I set a goal, I wonder *who* is going to do it. If it is not one of my special talents, I delegate it so that it gets done.

These are examples of what happens in a mentored life. This life is a joy.

I was over $1 million in debt because of a particularly bad decision. What did I do? I retained a mentor who was an expert in getting me out of debt.

Are you seeking mentors in all areas of your life in order to improve in areas that are important to you? This is your chance right now. This is your beginning. Look at your Annual Love Letters™, Life Missions™, Annual Backwards Goals™, Future Generator™, and MAINLY™ form. In which specific areas do you need assistance? In which specific areas do you need a mentor to move you forward?

On your own, you can do only what makes sense to you, but a mentor can provide you with ideas and thoughts that, although they might contradict what makes sense to you, actually might be much better.

You do what makes sense to you. Therefore, on your own, you keep doing the same thing all the time, because it makes sense to you. To have a giant leap forward in your life, you need to do what does *not* make sense to you. Only a very wise mentor can alert you to such new and strange actions you could take to make a huge change in your life.

Who's on Your Team?

What systems of accountability do you have in place? What will keep you on track and focused? How will you monitor your progress? Will you build a team to help support your vision? Share the ideas from this book with others in order to set up a system to support you and in turn help others to achieve their personal dreams and aspirations.

Talking with others makes your goals real. Share them with others! Set up a date and time to check in with updates on your progress. Set up a buddy system. It will give you the opportunity to share your hopes and dreams with another individual or group. It will give you the opportunity to have someone present you with a fresh perspective.

Connect with others to build a positive and supportive community around you. You could do this virtually (via e-mail or creating an online chat group) or by physically meeting at a local café. You could have one commitment buddy or you could work with a small group of likeminded individuals. Receiving recommendations or words of encouragement may be just what's needed to get you and keep you on track.

For example, if you have a commitment buddy to exercise with, you could make an agreement to jog at a certain time each day, whether it be meeting your buddy at the gym or having him knock on your door to jog in your neighborhood. What about making a little friendly competition to support each other—perhaps a little wager to make it fun? It could be number of pounds lost, if you have a common goal to lose weight. If you have to measure against some benchmark, you're guaranteed to accelerate your progress.

You can brainstorm together on ideas for rewards to feel great once you have achieved a goal. It may mean going on a trip, tickets to a show, going to a favorite restaurant, or going to a ballgame. Whatever the reward, sometimes a little friendly competition can go a long way to being a great motivator.

Yes, there will be cynics. Lurking out there are friends, family members, and colleagues who, unbeknownst to you, want you to stay exactly where you are now and do not want you to change. They may fear that, if you change, it will affect your relationship with them—and

> *"It is important that you recognize your progress and take pride in your accomplishments. Share your achievements with others. Brag a little. The recognition and support of those around you is nurturing."*
> —Rosemarie Rossetti

they are right. You need to be mindful of those around you. Build a strong and supportive community. If you notice that there are unsupportive people around you, then you may wish to record some MAINLY goals to bring supportive people into your life.

What happens when you start sliding in terms of not getting your MAINLY goals recorded each month? What happens when the naysayers begin to eat away at your positivity? What happens when you cannot find someone to handle a delegation? What happens when life throws you a fastball that hurts? What should you do in this case?

The answer lies in whether you have a supportive team around you and whether you have a mentor. If you have a team, seek solace from those wonderful, supportive souls. If you have a mentor, explain the situation to your mentor and get great advice. If you want a great mentor, I will give details on this later in the chapter.

Celebrate Your Successes

Notice your progress. Celebrate your achievements! Collect those wonderful souls around you who also share your excitement for your successes. It's a wonderful way to feel better about yourself and your progress. When you do, your self-esteem will skyrocket, and your self-esteem is the only weapon you have to succeed in this turbulent world.

Education is transient. Credentials are transient. They may stay with you, but they have less and less meaning as life goes on.

> *"Goals are a means to an end, not the ultimate purpose of our lives. They are simply a tool to concentrate our focus and move us in a direction. The only reason we really pursue goals is to cause ourselves to expand and grow. Achieving goals by themselves will never make us happy in the long term; it's who you become, as you overcome the obstacles necessary to achieve your goals that can give you the deepest and most long-lasting sense of fulfillment."*
> —Anthony Robbins

The value comes from a high self-esteem. Once you have high self-esteem you can achieve anything. The way to keep it high is not to attend motivational events. That lasts for a few hours. The only way to get the lasting benefit of increased self-esteem is to record goals and then to achieve them and then to notice and applaud your progress.

Raymond Is My Mentor

If you want me to be your mentor, simply go to www.aaron.com/DoubleYourIncome to find out how I can guide you to the place you wish to arrive at this month, this year, this lifetime. And, just for going there, I personally will send you a nice gift. Go there and find out what the gift is.

If I am your mentor, then you will faithfully:

- Do your MAINLY each month.
- Do your Annual Backwards Goals each year.
- Do your Annual Love Letters each year.
- Do your My Life Mission each year.

You will also faithfully:

- MTO all your goals.
- Select a delegation for each goal.
- Rely on advice from your mentor, whenever you need help.
- Clean messes each month.
- Acknowledge others each month.
- Increase your wealth each month.
- Do something new each month.
- Learn something each month.
- Do something just for you.
- Invoke the Law of Attraction so that the Universe does most of the work for you as you achieve your own goals.

You will also have:

- Considerable wisdom about delegation so that it will be easy for you to get help on your goals.
- A method for organizing your to-do list so that all those nagging incompletions actually get done.

- A process to overcome your toughest obstacles.
- A habit of invoking the Law of Attraction so that you get what you want in this lifetime.
- New supportive friends and colleagues who are positive and who will cheerlead you to success and wildly applaud your achievements.
- An overview of your life so that you work *on* your life instead of just *in* your life.
- A strategic vision for your life so that you move forward in the direction of your choice.
- And much, much more . . .

Does all this sound wonderful? It is—leading a mentored life is the only way to run a fulfilling life.

In a mentored life, you are the *director* of your own movie. You are the *author* of your autobiography. What will you produce—a comedy, a melodrama, a history? Yes, all this is within your ability to decide, no matter what you have, up till now, produced or failed to produce in your life.

Do you have lots of what you claim you do not want? Do you have smoking, debt, substance abuse, low income, relationship, or weight issues? You claim you do not want these. Yet, the Law of Attraction delivers what you have inadvertently requested, without your even realizing you requested it. You have been using the Law of Attraction backwards; it is now time, in a mentored life, to use the Law of Attraction correctly to truly get what you actually want.

This is the beginning of your new mentored life. Launch yourself powerfully into it through what you will learn at www.aaron.com/DoubleYourIncome.

Your Own Outrageous Successes

In my mentored program, the Monthly Mentor™, you will soon begin to have Outrageous successes. I want to know of your Outrageous successes. Please tell me all about them so that I can enjoy your progress. I have set up a special web site that I faithfully read because I get so turned on by the progress of my readers, members, and clients around the world.

Tell me all about your wildest accomplishments and your most outrageous successes at www.aaron.com/DoubleYourIncome.

You will soon eliminate your debt and skyrocket in your wealth. I want to know all about it.

You will soon have that lean, strong body you've been desiring. I want to know all about it.

You will soon have an orderly life, free of the messes that have plagued you. I want to know all about it. Please tell me. I am eager to be uplifted by your accomplishments.

Now it's your turn. It's your turn to select me as your mentor at www.aaron.com/DoubleYourIncome and to tell me soon about your Outrageous successes at www.aaron.com/DoubleYourIncome.

This is your beginning. It is the beginning of your new *mentored life*. Congratulations. I am your biggest cheerleader and your biggest fan.

APPENDIX

Testimonials from People Who Are Using the Principles of This Book

As a teenager, I was diagnosed clinically depressed. I dropped out of school. I spent two years in bed in my parents' home. Because I was so listless, I lost 35 pounds. I had no education, no future, no life, no hope, no income. Then I joined the Monthly Mentor™ and learned the amazing ideas taught in this book. Now, at age 22, I earn over $100,000 a year in my own business as Events Manager with clients across the country. I love my life. Thank you, Raymond.

Ryan Malfara
Events Manager

It's amazing the effect that Raymond has had on my life and my family. When we first met, my life was in shambles. Now, my income has more than tripled. I've bought over a million dollars' worth of rental real estate. I've started two businesses and feel younger than I have for years.

Dr. Bill Arkinstall
Medical Doctor

For over six years, I have been applying Raymond's goal-setting and goal-achieving strategies. I can sum them up in one word: brilliant. If you want to live with more success and fulfillment, then these strategies are a must.

Wayne Lee

Hypnotist

Raymond is a genius! His goal-setting methods are by far the most effective I have ever tried. It has changed the way I think. I have always been goal oriented, but somehow never set deadlines and timelines on achieving these goals. With Raymond's system, all I do is focus on goals, and I can proudly say I am accomplishing them. Thank you, Raymond.

Susan Kates

Owner of Dinnerworks

While many people understand the value of setting goals, few do it well. Raymond offers a lucid, well-thought-out guide to this important process. Who says you can't have the things you want right now? With Raymond's techniques, you can! His advice to do more by doing less sounds like a contradiction. It's actually a brilliant insight into the world of high achievers who focus their talents on the things they love to do, and delegate the rest! Now you can, too, with this straightforward guide to effective goal-setting.

Marco den Ouden

Author and TV News Coordinator

I had a gigantic and outrageous breakthrough doing the "Love Letters." It flowed out naturally and I realized I am going to achieve what was once distant and far away—completely outrageous loves I did not think I would ever achieve. The "My Life Mission" exercise flowed so easily, now that I have found my passion. I have new clarity and focus. I want everyone to feel, share, and experience the success I am enjoying. Without Raymond, *none* of this would be possible. I am very, very grateful. Being in an outrageous state feels like endless energy—and euphoric!

Dale Toffan

Municipal Employee

I have been working with Raymond's system for six months, and have already easily doubled my income. And, as far as I'm concerned,

I haven't even started. Because of Raymond's teachings, I have stepped through a door of endless possibilities. I am eternally grateful.

Ricke Verigin

Entrepreneur

The beauty of Raymond's goal-setting system is that, once they are recorded, it's as if the goals want to magically achieve themselves. This is because, unlike with any other program I've tried, my goals first and foremost tie into what I absolutely love most in life. The link between my daily to-do list and my life's dreams has never been stronger or clearer for me. Not only do I get things done, I know clearly in what direction I'm heading by doing them. Before, I felt like I had to push myself to accomplish little goals in front of me. Now I feel a magnetic pull to get through them to reach the powerful life dreams that lie at the end of their pathway. This system really works!

Michelle Anderson

Musician

Raymond, thank you for your goal-setting book and your guidance to achieve over 200 goals so far. Monthly I do more than six personal and six business goals. I just bought my first income property and paid off two major loans. I'm now focused on two major projects. I know where I am going in my life!

Bob Sim

Consultant and Investor

Raymond has developed a system that creates positive results. Using this system has allowed me to truly see where I want to be, and to achieve goals I thought were impossible.

Jane Atkins

Coach

Raymond Aaron has helped me laser-focus in on my passions, enabling me to make the transition from employee to running my own busy event-coordinating company. I've learned to design systems to keep my house, finances, and time in order; recognize fear and not allow it to immobilize my actions; and set big goals and conquer them with a step-by-step plan. I have steadily gained more confidence in my own abilities through Raymond's encouragements. His passion and insight have inspired me to achieve more, and share more with others. The most important skill I've learned is to do what I love, and delegate the rest. These goal-setting skills have made a huge change in the way I live and view the world.

Alice Zhou

Event Coordinator

After writing an outrageous goal of owning a house on a lake, I just bought my dream home—on a lake. Living and working here has been the happiest, most successful time of my life! I'm living my Dream Life! Thank you, Raymond.

Susan Bowman

Realtor

Raymond's outlook is refreshing and inspirational. His truth, clarity, and goal-setting program help you to discover who you truly hope to be and what you hope to accomplish. He then gives you the tools to joyfully become your vision. You will be inspired, motivated, and excited to grow into the person you are meant to be.

Dr. Jennifer Lee McGowan

Veterinarian, Juggler, and Unicyclist

It's amazing—in the 10 months since I adopted Raymond's incredible goal-setting methods, I'm having closer and more meaningful relationships with my wife and friends, I've doubled my business revenues and significantly raised my net worth, increased my physical strength and endurance limits, given more generously to charities, traveled more, laughed more, and learned more than ever before. Raymond has taught me how to do what I love, and in so doing I am at peace with my life and thrilled about my future!

Ray Liem

Accountant and Entrepreneur

When I began working with Raymond Aaron's program, I was ill with a rare disease and despondent about life. By taking the time to write down the goals to get me to my loves, slowly things turned around. I learned that the healing had to come from within—and guess what!—it did! I am excited to say that a mere 17 months later I am actually back at work! Thank you, Raymond.

Natalie Kanbergs

Aerospace Engineer

After using Raymond's system for less than two years, my income has quadrupled, I started two new businesses, and I have launched a successful career producing movies.

Simon Olszewski

Producer of Spiritual Movies

Raymond's amazing system of goal setting has, to my total astonishment, transformed every area of my life and lifted me to a completely new level of awareness. Using Raymond's system I have been able to eliminate all of the time-wasting messes in my life. Now my thoughts are clear and focused, allowing me to blast into the future with a clear vision of what I am doing on this earth, and why.

James E. McKinlay

Professional Travel Consultant

My life has been transformed since I began utilizing Raymond's goal-setting techniques three years ago. Reviewing my loves on a regular basis has had a great impact, bringing clarity and purpose to my goals and accomplishments. I have increased my earnings by 30 percent, bought the house of my dreams, and ended a draining relationship.

Val Mason

Arts and Culture Manager

In a heartbeat I received the biggest *ah-ha* of my life. I *got it!* Raymond's goal-setting methods worked instantly for me, leaving me breathless from accomplishing many of my Outrageous goals with ease.

Stanlie Hunt

President of The Smartstox Online TV Talk Show

Raymond's goal-setting program has added quality to my life by encouraging me to do only what I love. The program has helped me figure out I was frustrated because I no longer loved my job. Since beginning the program, I have resigned as a nurse. I have enrolled in postgraduate studies to accomplish my lifelong dream of teaching in my own nursing school. Now I am happier with my new job and my life, *and* I make more money!

Karima Sayani

Assistant Director of Nursing Care

It has been 35 months since I first committed to following Raymond's goal-setting program. Each month I record my goals on Raymond's special form as outlined in this book. As Raymond teaches, I keep a miniversion of my goals next to my Visa card in my wallet, which I thus see frequently. I have achieved great gains in terms of excitement in life, increase of assets, and, most notably, better relationships with my family, friends, and clients. I recommend this book to anyone who is serious about achieving their goals.

Kathy Elliott-Bryden

Raymond's precise program of goal setting provided a clear framework of organization to my life. It brought awareness to aspects that I may have neglected and serves as a constant reminder on a monthly basis, automatically. I'm more focused on being who I am, and doing what I love.

Chunkei Kenneth Chow

Architect

Raymond Aaron takes you on an incredible, methodical journey in your personal and professional life, allowing you to achieve goals you never would have imagined possible. His wisdom enables you to do the unreasonable, and settle for nothing less than the extraordinary!

Chris Downer

Police Sergeant

Raymond has made goal setting an amazing experience. The special monthly form that helped me clear up my credit mess, the Annual Backwards Goals, the Annual Love Letters, and, most powerful of all, My Life Missions all helped me form a vision as to where I wanted to go, what I needed to do to get there, and then how to celebrate my successes!

Brian Suliman

Infopreneur

It is so exciting to see my favorite mentor, Raymond Aaron, write a powerful book to share his wisdom with the world, because from Raymond I have learned more about following my dreams and taking action than from any other program in the past. I've learned that if I take action and do what most people are not willing to do, I will attain what most people simply dream of.

Chris Cumby

Entrepreneur

Raymond Aaron, unlike many others, has precisely defined the *setting of goals.* It is this precision that made my personal and business goals that much easier to achieve.

Dr. Arthur Dunec

Dentist

When I first met Raymond, my entire life had changed as a result of a divorce and relocation. I was faced with having to reengineer and rebuild my life. Working with Raymond's goal-setting strategies has given me an organized way of moving forward in my life, as well as hope for the future. I have been amazed at the rapid progress I have made when I score my monthly goals. The progress often seems quite effortless!

Kathleen Kennedy

Raymond's goal-setting program has brought back the 18-year-old Azita who was once full of joy, hope, and dreams. It saved me from severe depression, and it helped me rediscover the things I love that I'd long forgotten. I cleaned up a huge mess in my life, and I'm looking forward to so many other achievements for the years to come.

Azita Mafi

Legal Secretary

Following the recent loss of my wife to cancer, Raymond Aaron's goal-setting program has made a tremendous impact in my life. Being able to write down clear objectives, month after month, and seeing them fulfill themselves *automagically* has helped me rebuild my self-esteem. Now I am a single parent to two teenagers, and Raymond's system has guided me to plan my new future accordingly. Thank you, Raymond!

Fabrizio Patuelli

Engineer

I have been using Raymond's goal-setting strategies for three years. Raymond has helped me to personally accomplish more than twice what I did during the three years before that—not because I am smarter, but rather because I am more organized and focused on what matters to me. I expect my accomplishments for the next three years to grow even more rapidly.

Murray R. Mortlock

Power Engineer

Raymond's goal-setting principles are not only intellectually stimulating, but practically achievable. Setting six goals per month gives strong incentive to move forward in specific areas, and provide regular accountability. It sets a stage for success. We have been purchasing real estate for the past four years and know that action is key when we hear friends say they wish they could do the same. They could, but it takes courage; mentoring has been invaluable to us, providing the courage to act and not just wish.

Sharon and Ray Brubacher

Paralegal and Site Supervisor

Raymond's approach to goal setting brings even the greatest goals in life much closer to reality. After working with his system for 18 months, my husband and I have substantially increased our investments, own a rental property, and have created two new corporations with great profit potential. Through goal setting, most of this has happened *automagically*. I couldn't have wished to be in a better spot a year and a half ago. Thanks, Raymond!

Jacquie Millante

Project Manager

When I first met Raymond, I was down in the dumps, on medication, not knowing where my life was headed. I began working with his goal-setting program, and eight months later I have cleaned up my messes, planned my future, and started what I expect to be a *very* lucrative and fun new business, doing what I love. And no more pills! Thank you, Raymond!

Leonard Eagle

Entrepreneur

Raymond's goal-setting protocols have inspired me to visualize my dreams and my purpose in life, and to appropriately take action today to achieve results. His theory of working backwards from my year-end goal inspired me to take action today to achieve "that which I have already achieved." Equally important in Raymond's program is the concept of systematically cleaning up my financial mess so that I may proceed in doing more of the things I love. Raymond's program is definitely a groundbreaking approach to increasing my self-esteem and net worth in this unpredictable life.

Dominic Mastrocola

I am a fanatic about Raymond's program for achieving one's goals and loves in life. It has enabled me to double my six-figure income in less than 22 months, not to mention the huge strides I have made in my personal life. I've achieved a sense of accomplishment along with a concise understanding of how to keep the success in my life while doing only what I love. Raymond, thank you so much, and congratulations on getting this material out to anyone who truly wants to make a difference in their life.

Jim Scantland

Division Director

Through Raymond's program I have become a better communicator. I strive to have my inside match my outside, and I feel so free now, to just be myself.

Nicole Bhatia-Fellman

Small Business Administrator

Raymond has taken me from being a housewife to a successful businesswoman "doing what I love" in less than two years, by teaching me the process of sequential step-by-step goal setting. I've learned that the power of suggestion is unbelievable, and that when goals are written down, they can happen *automagically*. I now have 15 employees and a high-growth business.

Janice Douville
Businesswoman

I have used Raymond's forms as a goal-setting program every month for five years. It has helped me achieve clarity and balance by getting my messes cleaned up, and doing only what I love. I accomplish more through acknowledging rather than criticizing, by writing goals, particularly long-term ones, giving extra-good service, and then letting the good things happen. Thank you, Raymond.

Jo Blackmore
Book Publisher

Raymond Aaron offers a clear, precise, and practical approach to goal setting and follow-up. This inspiring and self-motivating method has enabled me to grow tremendously over the past year. Raymond and his support team have offered me the tools to elevate myself to the next level, surrounding myself with what I love.

James Nienhuis
President, The Butler Did It

Raymond's methods of setting goals and his ways of working toward them and achieving them *automagically* (a word that he created) are really inconceivable. In the first three months I set and achieved so many goals that previously I would never have been able achieve in three *years*. Thank you, Raymond!

Aziz Amiri

I've had your goal-setting material for a week and I can already say with confidence that this is the greatest program I have ever seen. I'm going over each section about five times to ensure I have a good foundation, and it has already allowed me to look at life in a new and better way. If the rest of the program continues to have such an impact, you will surely have a success story for the ages.

Gerry Hayes
Restaurant Owner and Real Estate Investor

After working with Raymond's program for only nine months, I have accomplished things that until now I only dreamed about—like learning to play the piano at age 38. Cleaning up many personal messes has been huge in moving me closer to my dreams. My newly organized home office inspires me to go after the things that I really want out of life, like changing my career. My goal is to at least double my income in the next 12 months doing only what I love. I'm so grateful for Raymond's program. World, look out—here I come!

Joseph Neff

Setting goals is one thing; achieving them is another. Raymond's system uses the great truth of good business strategy—systematization—to put your goal achieving on autopilot. In the last few months, Raymond's methodology has helped me change from just a property investor. I downsized my property landlording focus, and became a business strategist and coach/mentor. I am now working in all three asset classes of business, property, and derivative trading. Raymond's ideas helped me gain a handle on this transition, with purposed vision, in a relatively short time.

Rafe Vanderwall

This book inspires you to greatness, with a practical approach to achieving your dreams. Raymond's masterful lessons are presented in an easy-flowing way. Just act upon what he presents and your success is assured. Every chapter offers excitement, passion, valuable insights, and a practical approach to improving your life.

Ken Ballard
Professional Speaker and Business Coach

Raymond has figured out the fastest and easiest way to accomplish your wildest fantasies. His MTO technique is revolutionary.

Never have I seen it before, and it has changed my life forever by allowing me to consistently achieve my goals.

Philippe Desrochers

Salesman and Professional Speaker

I have achieved outrageous results in my life—like doubling my income in one year—by using the tools of this book for 30 minutes per month.

George Fabi

Real Estate Investor

About The Author

One of the most exciting and sought-after speakers in North America, **Raymond Aaron** has committed his life to teaching people just like you how to utilize his amazing, proven wealth-creation systems to double, triple, and even quadruple their income. Raymond's highly innovative techniques and strategies show you how to take total conscious control of your life so you can spend more time doing *only* what you love to do—and making more money than you ever dreamed possible.

Raymond reveals these fast-track success strategies in programs such as The Monthly Mentor™, The Wealth Creator Source™, and The Real Estate Wiz™.

Renowned for his passion for and total commitment to his clients, Raymond seizes every opportunity to demonstrate the power of his teachings, teachings he himself lives by each and every day. At the young age of 62, he recently (April 2007) completed a 350-mile, month-long footrace to the North Pole, hauling a 100-pound sled containing all his provisions and braving temperatures as low as –68°—a truly amazing feat by any standard.

Raymond is co-author of the Canadian bestselling *Chicken Soup for the Canadian Soul* and the *New York Times* Top-Ten Bestselling *Chicken Soup for the Parent's Soul*. He has appeared on hundreds of radio and TV programs throughout the United States and Canada. He delivers 200 presentations a year on his favorite topics of mentoring, and of setting and achieving your goals. For more information on Raymond, please visit the following web sites:

www.aaron.com

www.MonthlyMentor.com

www.WealthCreatorSource.com

www.TheRealEstateWiz.com

www.ChickenSoupForTheParentsSoul.com

www.ChickenSoupForTheCanadianSoul.com

Index